Cambridge Elements

Elements in International Relations
edited by
Jon C. W. Pevehouse
University of Wisconsin–Madison
Tanja A. Börzel
Freie Universität Berlin
Edward D. Mansfield
University of Pennsylvania

TIP-TOEING THROUGH THE TULIPS WITH CONGRESS

How Congressional Attention Constrains Covert Action

Dani Kaufmann Nedal
University of Toronto

Madison V. Schramm
University of Toronto

CAMBRIDGE
UNIVERSITY PRESS

Shaftesbury Road, Cambridge CB2 8EA, United Kingdom

One Liberty Plaza, 20th Floor, New York, NY 10006, USA

477 Williamstown Road, Port Melbourne, VIC 3207, Australia

314–321, 3rd Floor, Plot 3, Splendor Forum, Jasola District Centre, New Delhi – 110025, India

103 Penang Road, #05–06/07, Visioncrest Commercial, Singapore 238467

Cambridge University Press is part of Cambridge University Press & Assessment, a department of the University of Cambridge.

We share the University's mission to contribute to society through the pursuit of education, learning and research at the highest international levels of excellence.

www.cambridge.org
Information on this title: www.cambridge.org/9781009598002

DOI: 10.1017/9781009598019

First published 2024

A catalogue record for this publication is available from the British Library.

ISBN 978-1-009-59800-2 Hardback
ISBN 978-1-009-59799-9 Paperback
ISSN 2515-706X (online)
ISSN 2515-7302 (print)

Cambridge University Press & Assessment has no responsibility for the persistence or accuracy of URLs for external or third-party internet websites referred to in this publication and does not guarantee that any content on such websites is, or will remain, accurate or appropriate.

Tip-toeing through the Tulips with Congress

How Congressional Attention Constrains Covert Action

Elements in International Relations

DOI: 10.1017/9781009598019
First published online: December 2024

Dani Kaufmann Nedal
University of Toronto

Madison V. Schramm
University of Toronto

Author for correspondence: Dani Kaufmann Nedal, dani.nedal@utoronto.ca

Abstract: Over the years, the US has intervened covertly in many countries to remove dictators, subvert elected leaders, and support coups. Existing work tends to focus on the characteristics of target countries or the strategic incentives to pursue regime change. This Element provides an account of the domestic political factors constraining US presidents' use of covert foreign-imposed regime change operations (FIRCs). We argue that congressional attention to covert action alters the Executive's calculus by increasing the political costs and operational risks associated with this secretive policy instrument. We also show that congressional attention is primarily the result of institutional battles over abuses of executive authority and has a significant constraining effect independent of codified rules and partisan disputes. We test our argument using content analysis of the Congressional Record, statistical models of Cold War covert FIRCs, and causal-process evidence relating to covert interventions in Chile, Angola, Central America, Afghanistan, and beyond.

Keywords: covert action, domestic politics of foreign policy, foreign-imposed regime change, US foreign policy, executive–legislative relations

ISBNs: 9781009598002 (HB) 9781009597999 (PB) 9781009598019 (OC)
ISSNs: 2515-706X (online), 2515-7302 (print)

Contents

1 Introduction

Since the CIA was created from the skeleton of the Office of Strategic Services in 1947, US presidents have used it to destabilize, depose, and/or shore up governments around the world (Leary, 1984; Durbin, 2017; O'Rourke, 2018). Covert operations aimed at foreign-imposed regime change (FIRC) have relied on methods ranging from assassination to massive campaigns of political interference and psychological warfare, and have been a part of every administration since Harry Truman's tenure.

The literature on foreign intervention has flourished in the past two decades.[1] Initially, most of this work centered on conventional, overt military interventions, leaving covert activities understudied. Recent work has started to change this state of affairs, exploring various facets of covert interventions and showing that secretive operations are far more ubiquitous than their overt counterparts.[2] This new scholarship has generally focused on the *effects* – or effectiveness – of these covert interventions and the demand-side logic of intervention; that is, the characteristics of target countries, dyadic relationships between initiator and target, or strategic reasoning behind particular interventions. Although there are various reasons individual interventions have been pursued, such as opening markets (Berger et al., 2013), concern over democratic erosion (Poznansky, 2015), or loss of influence (O'Rourke, 2018), existing work largely overlooks the *supply side* of the equation – how domestic politics in the United States creates an environment that favors or constrains the use of covert tools to promote regime change abroad. This can be attributed largely to extensive scholarship documenting challenges inherent in the oversight of covert operations and intelligence. Zegart (2011), for example, argues that weak political incentives for representatives to develop expertise coupled with challenges in leveraging budgetary power make effective oversight exceedingly difficult. Zegart and Quinn (2010) also highlight how the dearth of intelligence-related interest groups creates obstacles to effective oversight. Durbin (2017) argues that reform is most likely when political agreement regarding national security is particularly low and Congress can overcome informational asymmetries, a rare combination. Even Colaresi (2014), who is more sanguine about the effectiveness of legislative influence

---

[1] See, for example, Krasner (2009); Wheeler (2000); Westad et al. (2005); Saunders (2009); Kuperman (2008); Pickering and Kisangani (2009); Peksen (2011); Petersen (2011); Murdie and Peksen (2014); Howard and Stark (2018); Bueno de Mesquita and Downs (2006); Biddle et al. (2012).

[2] Levin (2016); Poznansky (2015); Carson (2018); Downes and O'Rourke (2016); O'Rourke (2018); Poznansky et al. (2017); Smith (2019); Durbin (2017); Downes (2021); Wohlforth (2020).

over national security, suggests that even in countries with relatively stronger oversight institutions it may be impossible to deter abuses, as executives can learn and adapt to avoid exposure. While this scholarship provides important insights into the challenges of oversight, it may have led scholars to drastically underestimate the role of domestic politics in constraining US covert activities.

Synthesizing insights from International Relations, American Politics, and History, and marshaling a mix of quantitative and qualitative evidence, pairing computer-assisted content analysis of Congressional Records and statistical analysis of covert operations with causal-process observations from multi-archival primary sources, we identify and demonstrate the powerful constraining effects of congressional *attention* on the use of covert means to overthrow foreign regimes. We argue that legislative attention to intelligence and covert action substantially alters Executive decision-making by increasing the perception of costs and risks associated with these foreign policy instruments. As such, we complement existing *demand-side explanations* of covert intervention and contribute to a recently reinvigorated research agenda on the domestic politics of US foreign policy.[3]

This Element proceeds in six sections. In the remainder of this section, we briefly review existing studies that quantify and allow us to map variation in covert FIRC activity over time and introduce our theory on the constraining effect of congressional attention, noting our contribution to the broader scholarship on the politics of American foreign policy. Section 2 offers a brief historical overview and explanation for early patterns in congressional attention (or lack thereof). In Section 3, we introduce a quantitative measure of attention using content analysis of Congressional Records and subsequently use this measure to test our hypothesis that heightened attention produces fewer instances of FIRCs operations. Section 4 illustrates our proposed causal processes, addresses potential competing explanations, and evaluates modeling assumptions using case-study evidence of decision-making over CIA involvement in Angola, as well as additional causal-process evidence from late Cold War decisions regarding covert interventions in Central America and Northern Africa.[4] Section 5 extends the analysis to the "secret" war in Afghanistan, a case commonly associated with congressional *support* for covert action, and illustrates how heightened congressional attention can act as a constraint on covert operations *even when legislators do not intend it to*. Together, the cases

---

[3] See for example Howell and Pevehouse (2007); Kriner (2010, 2018); Peck and Jenkins (2020); Kreps (2010); Kreps and Das (2017); Tama (2024); Saunders (2024).

[4] Our methodological approach here is inspired by what Seawright (2016) calls integrative multi-method.

in Sections 4 and 5 provide strong evidence of how variation in congressional attention affected the calculus of decision-makers in the Executive and led to profound changes in whether, how, and how much covert action was used to advance US interests around the world. The final section concludes with a discussion, suggestions for further research, and implications for current policy.

1.1 Temporal Variation in US Covert Activities

Identifying instances of covert FIRCs is a notoriously difficult task given the secretive nature of the subject matter. The task is also complicated by definitional disagreements regarding both covert action and regime change itself, with scholars disagreeing on what counts as sufficient involvement to warrant a case being considered an US-backed attempt at regime change. Setting aside these disagreements, we can identify common trends by examining patterns across different studies by Levin (2016), O'Rourke (2018), Berger et al. (2013), and Johnson (1989). Figure 1 depicts the patterns in the first two datasets by Levin and O'Rourke, illustrating that covert interventions peaked in the 1950s and 1960s and reached their nadir in the mid-to-late 1970s, before surging again in the Reagan administration. Importantly, in both datasets the sharp decrease in activity *precedes* the institutional reforms and oversight overhaul of 1973–75.

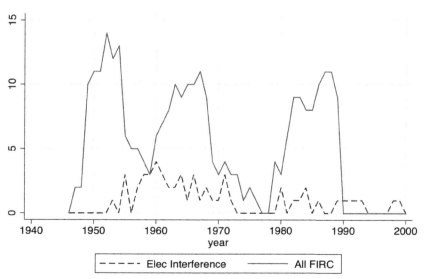

Figure 1 Covert electoral interference (Levin) and covert FIRCs (O'Rourke).

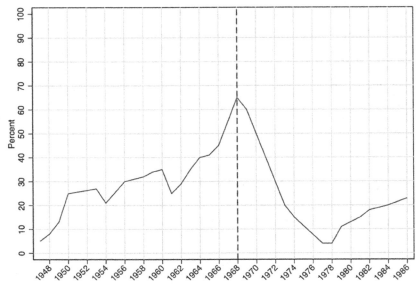

Figure 2 % of CIA annual budget dedicated to covert action (approx.),
reconstructed from Johnson (1989, 103).

This general pattern is similar to the one found by Berger et al., who identify cases where the CIA removed "an existing leader and installed a new leader" (Berger et al., 2013, 867) from 1945 to 1989. While the authors note a gradual decline in *active* influence operations starting in the late 1960s, their dataset only includes one instance of a *new* operation between 1969 and 1981. This pattern is also largely consistent with Loch Johnson's estimates of the CIA's operations budget from 1947 to 1986, represented in Figure 2, which pinpoints an apex of expenditures in the late 1960s, a sharp decline starting in 1968–69, and an uptick after 1979 (Johnson, 1989, 87).

As we argue in the following sections, existing explanations focusing either on international factors, such as the rise and fall of detente, or domestic-political factors, such as partisan opposition or formal reform, struggle to account for this variation, especially these specific inflection points and the reversal in the 1980s. While most existing IR studies of US covert action acknowledge, even if in passing, the importance of the investigations and hearings in the early-to-mid 1970s and subsequent reforms, few attempt to more systematically theorize how changes in domestic politics affect the dynamics of covert FIRCs. Our theory suggests that rather than being a one-off chain of events or shocks that definitively and irrevocably changed the policy environment, effective constraints on presidential behavior are largely the product of sustained congressional attention and that this attention can wax and wane even after reforms are instituted, as formal rules and regulations can be undone or circumvented.[5]

1.2 How Congressional Attention Constrains FIRCs

The battle between the Executive and Congress regarding control and authority over different policy instruments is well documented, and scholars have long noted that it is a perennial struggle that nevertheless varies greatly in intensity over time. This research has shown that there are inherent challenges for congressional assertiveness on foreign policy, but that this does not mean that Congress is powerless against the president even in matters of national security (Lindsay, 1994; Howell and Pevehouse, 2007; Fowler, 2015). Much of the recent scholarship on democratic foreign policy has focused on the role of "domestic audience costs," or the political costs that the general public, or at least the *attentive public* can impose on leaders in a democratic society (Fearon, 1994; Schultz, 2001; Davies and Johns, 2013). Scholars such as Jessica Weeks and Elizabeth Saunders have shown that elites can constitute their own set of relevant audiences even when the public is inattentive or unable to hold leaders directly accountable (Weeks, 2008; Saunders, 2015). Others have argued that elites play an important role in *mediating* the effect of mass opinion, by shaping or "cueing" public beliefs (Page and Shapiro, 2010; Guisinger and Saunders, 2017), or by acting as "filters" through which public opinion is interpreted and acted upon (Foyle, 1997). Saunders explains that "[l]eaders can retain significant autonomy to conduct foreign policy – including foolish or losing policies – as long as an elite consensus holds, or elite dissent is contained" (Saunders, 2012, 3). One of our contributions in this volume is to argue how the influence of political elites, particularly members of the US Congress, is at least partly conditional on their *paying attention* to certain foreign policy issues. Attention is a scarce resource and, therefore, an important

---

[5] Franck and Weisband (1979) argued that the institutional reforms of the 1970s constituted a "revolutionary moment" for congressional constraints on US foreign policy. While this period brought discussion of US covert action into the elite and public discourse, the constraining effects were not permanent. Franck and Weisband, as we show, were overly optimistic that the dynamics at the time of their writing would be sustained. The variety of mechanisms they attributed to Congress' new influence in foreign affairs – such as increased levels of congressional activism, interest in foreign policy, capacity, and the larger political culture regarding US adventurism – fluctuated significantly over time and were unable to fully counteract the effect of structural changes and presidential preferences in the years to follow. As we demonstrate next, just in the few years following the publication of their book, congressional attention to covert action declined, before increasing again in the mid-1980s. This is consistent with Franck and Weisband's broader point that power over foreign policy can shift in both directions, not only from Congress to the president but also from the president to Congress, as it did after the Jackson presidency, and, to some extent, after Wilson's second term.

indicator of political priorities (Jones and Baumgartner, 2004). Legislators, like all political actors, must pick and choose how they spend their limited time and cognitive resources, and what issues they choose to focus on at any given time. We draw on multi-archival research to offer compelling causal-process evidence that legislators' ability to influence foreign policy is partly determined by where their attention lies and that both legislators and policy-makers in the Executive are acutely aware of these dynamics.

Our research builds on scholarship from Howell and Pevehouse (2007), Peck and Jenkins (2020), Kriner (2010, 2018), and Tama (2020, 2024), among others, in showing *how* legislators can influence foreign policy through formal and, especially, informal mechanisms. As scholars of American politics have noted, legislators spend their valuable and scarce time not only on introducing and passing legislation but also on various other activities meant to shape policy and increase their influence and power, either individually or institutionally. As Josh Chafetz argues, "Congress has numerous powers other than the power to pass bills into law, powers that tend to receive scant treatment even in isolation; they are almost never grouped together and conceptualized as a coherent set of legislative tools. And yet these tools together are potent, giving Congress the ability to assert itself vigorously against the other branches" (Chafetz, 2017, 2). This is also one of the central arguments in Mayhew's seminal work on congressional behavior. He notes that "Members of Congress perform actions beyond just making laws […] [they] take part in the public sphere in an impressive variety of other ways. […] As important as anything, perhaps, they take stands" (Mayhew, 2000, 227). James Lindsay, in his study of congressional influence over foreign policy, devotes an entire chapter to nonlegislative activities designed to influence public and elite opinion and consequently shape policy (Lindsay, 1994). This broader range of actions can increase the costs to the executive after a policy is implemented as well as affect how they anticipate the costs associated with future actions (Howell and Pevehouse, 2007). For example, Kriner found experimental evidence that "Legislatures need not necessarily exercise their constitutional war powers to influence the conduct of military affairs" (Kriner, 2018, 64). In particular, he contends that congressional criticism can greatly affect popular support for military action and the Commander-in-Chief, thus constraining the president.

While there is a rich scholarship on how Congress and other political elites can constrain or influence presidential decisions regarding overt military action and other national security issues such as alliance formation and defense expenditures, few studies have explored how these instruments affect the calculus related to covert action. There is good reason for this. It is reasonable to expect that some of these challenges Congress faces in influencing foreign policy are particularly acute in the realm of intelligence and covert action: Congress faces a substantial information asymmetry – even more than in other areas – legislators are unlikely to benefit electorally from pursuing oversight over intelligence, classification regulations and practices create barriers for information sharing, and interest groups and lobby activities are relatively scarce even at the height of scandals, leading experts to expect this to be an issue area where the Executive should have a particularly easy time retaining autonomy (Zegart, 2013; Colaresi, 2014; Milner and Tingley, 2015).

Two recent studies have made important progress in excavating the effects of domestic politics on covert action and testing them empirically. Nandita Balakrishnan (2020) argues that institutional reforms in Congress, following a spate of scandals in the early 1970s, severely limited US ability to intervene abroad to support coups, causing a decline in military coup activity around the world. In another recent study, Gregory Smith (2019) argues that prior to these oversight reforms in the 1970s, patterns in US covert operations were best explained by partisan opposition in divided governments. Once oversight mechanisms are in place, however, he suggests that divided government plays a diminished role, or perhaps none at all. We argue that these studies are correct in highlighting the potential for domestic politics to affect the resort to covert action, but that neither tells a complete story and both fail to capture the central role that congressional attention, flawed and uneven though it may be, plays in reining in the president's use of covert operations.

An account that focuses on partisan opposition[6] and divided government struggles to explain the exuberant use of covert FIRCs by the Eisenhower administration and the muted congressional response to those operations at a time when Democrats held both the House and Senate, as well as pitched battles over executive overreach in covert operations after reforms took place.[7] In the absence of sustained elite attention, early attempts at strengthening congressional oversight (pushed largely – but not solely – by liberal Democrats under Republican and Democratic presidencies) were met with intransigence and foot-dragging by the White House as well as by a broad bipartisan consensus that produced, by both omission and commission, what historiographies of US intelligence consider the golden age of legislative deference to the intelligence

---

[6] Partisan opposition is what Frances Lee calls "partisan teamshmanship" or "partisan bickering," disputes that are driven not by substantive disagreement over policy or principle, but by the electorally motivated need to challenge, undermine, or embarrass their opponents in the pursuit of office and power (Lee, 2009, 2016).

[7] Eisenhower authorized more FIRCs than any other president during the Cold War, even though Democrats regained control of both the House and the Senate in 1956 and held it through the end of his presidency.

community and the Executive and what proponents of executive autonomy call the period of "benign neglect."[8]

Similarly, an emphasis on institutional reforms and formal oversight cannot explain the downward trend in covert FIRCs in the late 1960s to early 1970s, before new oversight mechanisms were instituted, nor can it explain the later increase in the 1980s, when many of the formal mechanisms were still in place. We do not argue that formal oversight or codified rules, such as the creation of the Senate and House Select Committees on Intelligence or the Foreign Intelligence Surveillance Act were unimportant. Whereas Zegart and Quinn (2010) have argued that congressional oversight is generally ineffective "by design," we suggest that the effectiveness of these mechanisms is somewhat conditional on the level of congressional attention and that attention itself can have a powerful constraining effect even when formal oversight mechanisms are poorly institutionalized.[9]

Covert and clandestine activities tend to have an affinity with executive autonomy, as they rely on remaining secret and/or deniable – this is, in fact, their defining trait. As such, widespread attention or publicity, whether supportive or critical, can constitute a major threat to covert operations, especially when coming from recognizable official sources.[10] A key implication is that covert activities are *particularly vulnerable* to nonlegislative actions by members of Congress such as floor speeches, press releases, leaks, and hearings. In other words, when it comes to covert action, broad congressional attention is not only an indicator of *potential* political costs or constraints but can also *directly* produce risks and costs for the Executive and its agents.

To explore congressional attention and its associated effects on the president's authorization of FIRCs, we introduce, in the following sections, evidence from computer-assisted content analysis of Congressional Records, statistical analysis of covert operations, and causal-process observations from multi-archival primary sources. Following Quinn et al. (2010), we operationalize congressional attention by examining how often a legislator talks about an issue on the Congress floor.[11] Speeches, we argue, offer an

---

[8] Critics would disagree with the "benign" characterization, while agreeing with the "neglect."

[9] This is closer to the argument that oversight mechanisms operate more like "fire alarms" than "police patrols." See Johnson (2005); McCubbins and Schwartz (1984). However, we also show that presidents and congressional supporters of executive autonomy worked hard to prevent Congress from "patrolling the streets" or at least to keep the number of patrols down to a minimum, as it were.

[10] For some recent literature on the tensions between covert action and publicity, see, for example, Colaresi (2014); Aronsson-Storrier (2020); Joseph and Poznansky (2018); Cormac and Aldrich (2018); Carnegie and Carson (2020); Eason et al. (2020).

[11] For a similar measure see Hughes (2018).

imperfect but less biased measure of what issues members of Congress consider worthy of attention and, importantly, what they consider worthy of *public* consumption.[12] Because floor speeches are public, taking something to the floor enters it in the official record and carries the likelihood that it will be picked up by other members of Congress, the media, or other interested parties. While committee hearings or bills, which other studies have used to measure the intensity of congressional interest in a topic, are potentially a more costly signal of priority and position, they can also be kept behind closed (sub)committee doors, redacted, and "sanitized" before being released to the public, as is the case with much of congressional activity on matters of intelligence and covert action. We show throughout this volume that administration officials and congressional supporters of executive autonomy have understood this of floor debates and have tried to prevent or quell them accordingly.

While we do not discount bills, resolutions, or hearings in our qualitative account of the fights over congressional oversight, there are also methodological reasons to favor floor speeches over these other instruments: they are more subject to systematic bias due to correlation with other variables of interest like partisanship and institutional capacity. Precisely because hearings and bills are time-consuming to organize and draft, they are much more reliant on the existence of committee staff, which means that we are far more likely to observe these after dedicated committees were established in the mid-1970s. If partisan opposition plays a role in attention and oversight, hearings and bills will be a very biased measure, less likely to be observed in times of unified government as majority parties are expected to block hearings and votes that they deem prejudicial to their president or preferred policies.

This is not to suggest that we expect partisanship or partisan opposition to be the main driver of legislative activity on intelligence and covert action – and as we show later it is not – only to guard against potential measurement bias as it relates to possible alternative explanations. As Zegart notes, "lackluster intelligence oversight from the 1940s to the 1970s remained remarkably resilient and consistent despite changes in party control of the House and Senate, despite fourteen years of unified government and sixteen years of divided government, and despite nearly an even split between Democratic and Republican presidents "(Zegart, 2013, 22). Nor are we suggesting that low polarization or a supposed "bipartisan Cold War consensus" meant that politics stopped at the water's edge.[13] Rather, we argue that politics was very much an important

---

[12] For another example of recent research that operationalizes attention through speech acts see Froio et al. (2017).

[13] Milner and Tingley (2015).

part of foreign policy-making during the Cold War, but that not all politics is partisan, and that Legislative attempts to reel in executive power transcended partisan divides even as polarization deepened. Our argument in this Element is in line with recent work that calls into question binary and static conceptions of partisanship and the tendency to read current partisan divides and levels of polarization back into the historical record, inadvertently exaggerating or misunderstanding its role (Friedrichs and Tama, 2022).

We also draw on scholars such as Gries (2020) and Jeong and Quirk (2019) who suggest that ideology, aside and apart from – and maybe more so than – partisanship, plays a critical role in explaining congressional preferences over foreign policy. Our qualitative and quantitative analysis both speak to the importance of disentangling ideology and partisanship in this way to understand the fault lines over covert action, intelligence, and executive authority during the Cold War – and perhaps beyond.[14] We also find, consistent with other recent scholarship, that presidents often worry more about co-partisan than about opposition critics.[15] A recent study focusing specifically on congressional oversight of intelligence notes that "for Congress to impose its will over the executive's preferences [...], members of Congress from the president's party must also agree that the executive's relationship to the CIA needs restructuring" (Haas, 2023, 8). Tama refers to this as anti-presidential bipartisanship – the cooperation between the two major parties to constrain or oppose presidential policies – and finds that even in today's extremely polarized environment, bipartisanship is more common than traditionally recognized on matters of foreign policy (Tama, 2024).

To be sure, some studies have found that the partisan composition of Congress can affect US foreign and security policy and that opposition politics can be a constraint on the president. For example, Kriner finds that when a president is faced with less partisan support, they are less likely to use force abroad (Kriner, 2010), and Howell and Pevehouse (2007) demonstrate that when leaders face strong majority opposition, they issue fewer executive orders. These effects, even on overt action, however, are not universal but contingent. Howell and Pevehouse (2007) further find that the composition of Congress matters only for major uses of force and not for minor deployments.[16] This is consistent with our expectation and findings that partisanship plays a smaller role when considering covert operations that are usually far cheaper

---

[14] In the Appendix, we show evidence that ideology predicts attention to intelligence oversight better than partisanship, with liberal Democrats and Republicans being consistently more likely to speak out on the issue relative to their more conservative counterparts.

[15] See for example Baum and Groeling (2009); Wells and Ryan (2018); Tama (2024).

[16] Cf. Gowa (1998) and Fordham (2002), who find no such effect on US use of military force.

and have a much smaller physical footprint than even the most limited overt military operations. We also find evidence that the extent to which intelligence and covert action matters become polarized across party lines is itself partially a product of how much attention these issues get, both within Congress and among the broader public. This means that politicians have a degree of choice in how much they want fights over covert action to become partisan issues and that they often choose the mode and venue of the fight accordingly, to either minimize or maximize polarization.

The resulting picture is one in which congressional attention affects executive decisions regarding covert action independently from formally codified oversight, and, second, that congressional attention is not a manifestation of partisan disputes or simply a reflection of opposition politics, or a purely reactive or opportunistic response to policy failures or scandals. We propose that congressional attention creates particular problems for covert operations, namely making it difficult to keep them covert, raising the expected political costs and risks associated with these operations.

2 Understanding Congressional Attention to Covert Action

In this section we focus on the variation in congressional attention to covert action between 1947 and the late nineteen seventies and on the early attempts at strengthening congressional oversight. While providing a full account of the history of oversight or an in-depth analysis of the *drivers* of congressional attention to covert operations is outside the scope of this Element,[17] we point to a few critical variables and specific events that affected congressional attention, address measurement issues, and explore possible sources of endogeneity. In doing so, we establish a few important points in the pages that follow. First, congressional attention to covert operations and the associated costs to the executive fluctuate substantially over time. While existing work tends to identify two periods, divided by the intelligence reforms of 1974–1975, we show that attention varied substantially within each of those periods and that this variation helps explain meaningful changes in the incidence, the intensity, and the form of covert operations over time. We offer evidence of an early bipartisan consensus not only *against* establishing firmer oversight of the CIA, but also against allowing the issue to become a topic of wider conversation *within Congress*, not to mention the broader public, even after widely publicized CIA-related blunders. Most legislators, other elites, and even the broader public were

---

[17] For historical accounts, see Snider (2015); Theoharis et al. (2005); Jeffreys-Jones (2003). For more analytical accounts, see Zegart (2013); Lester (2015); Durbin (2017); Johnson (2017). Future work can further refine and interrogate the sources of attention.

little bothered by the lack of oversight of covert operations, even when things went wrong. The prevailing attitude was expressed by Everett Dirksen, Republican Senate Minority Leader, in 1966: "There will be mistakes . . . But you've got to accept the mistakes. You can't discuss them." The covert action cases that did draw attention in the late 1960s and early 1970s were perceived by the White House and the intelligence community not as errors or excesses to avoid, but as normal and necessary, as revealed by discussions among administration officials.

Second, and related, we highlight how the most important early battles over executive discretion and congressional oversight were triggered by revelations regarding *domestic* espionage, propaganda, and surveillance, and other abuses that incidentally uncovered CIA propaganda and paramilitary operations abroad; as well as scandals linked to foreign intelligence gathering and *overt* military action, in places like the Dominican Republic and, of course, Vietnam. Perceived overreach in executive authority and violations of established democratic principles and statutes, be they associated with tragic policy blunders or successes, affected the visibility and the salience of the CIA among political elites, the media, and the mass public. This increased publicity provided legislators with not only a mandate and incentives to exercise tighter control over the Agency but also with a more powerful platform to expose government secrets, including covert operations that would not have received sustained attention or opposition on their own. These two points echo repeatedly throughout the rest of the Element: perhaps the thorniest and most consistently divisive issues regarding oversight were not the questions of constitutional authority, the morality of specific forms of covert action, or the financial cost of the operations, but one of who should have access to details of covert operations and when and how to prevent them from leaking or willfully disclosing that information.

Third, we highlight that the break in the bipartisan consensus against discussing intelligence and covert action publicly arose not from partisan opposition, but primarily as a manifestation of ideological and institutional battles, with liberals leading the charge in the campaign for oversight regardless of who occupied the Oval Office.

This section also illustrates how attention sometimes took time to mount, as oversight advocates needed to overcome information asymmetries and mobilize key allies and audiences, but other times increased rapidly as a response to specific events. Some of these abrupt spikes in attention came after revelations made on the floor of Congress, others by news stories based on leaks, many of which came from congressmen or their staff. Some of these were multi-part stories in major newspapers. Others were broken by dogged reporters writing in minor publications. In that sense, some of the broader attention was endogenous or intentionally caused by legislators themselves. In important ways, congressional attention to and interest in oversight of intelligence and covert operations is partly a function of broader disputes over executive authority writ large and Congress' role in foreign policy in particular. As such, some of the variation in congressional attention we explore herein can be explained by the same structural causes and culmination of major events well known for contributing to those broader institutional battles. But even as we appreciate the importance of these structural factors and how they created a more permissive or constraining environment, we should not lose sight of the importance of individuals and contingencies.[18]

As Howell and Pevehouse note, by deciding to intervene in the Korean Peninsula without seeking congressional approval, Truman marked the beginning of an era of diminished congressional influence over foreign policy (Howell and Pevehouse, 2007, 3).[19] By the 1970s, executive power in the realm of foreign policy had reached a crescendo in what historian Arthur Schlesinger would refer to as the "imperial presidency" (Schlesinger, 2004). Although it is difficult to identify a single inflection point in elite attention, several changes in the 1960s and 1970s began to alter the balance of power between the branches. Support for the Vietnam War dropped, particularly following the Tet Offensive, among Congress and the US population writ large; and deference to the national security establishment began to wane (Franck and Weisband, 1979; Howell and Pevehouse, 2007; Kupchan and Trubowitz, 2007). Trubowitz and Kupchan argue that heightened perceptions of external threats correspond with greater deference to the Executive on foreign policy (Kupchan and Trubowitz, 2007) and that, as tensions between the United States and the Soviet Union cooled in 1969, the threat environment relaxed. Additionally, a shift can be identified in judicial decision-making in the late 1960s and early 1970s favoring government transparency (Lester, 2015, 57). The associated informational dynamics and electoral incentives also shifted, signaling a move away from unquestioned executive dominance over certain policy areas. Ultimately, these processes were not independent but likely reinforced one another to create an

---

[18] For a powerful call on political scientists to take seriously the causal effects of events, see Mayhew (2000). We focus not only on specific legislators and presidents but also CIA directors, who can play an equally important role depending on their own dispositions and preferences but also how well or poorly they managed CIA–Congress relations. Lester and Jones (Lester and Jones, 2021), for example, point to the role DCI William Colby played in the chain of events that led to the Hughes-Ryan Amendment.

[19] While the United States emerged as a superpower after the Second World War and possessed more *capacity* to engage in large military actions overseas, breaking free of these institutional constraints was necessary to employ that newfound power.

environment more conducive to congressional constraints on US foreign policy. This can also help explain the corresponding decrease in congressional authority in these matters in the early 1980s, following the Soviet invasion of Afghanistan and the collapse of detente.

In general terms, executive autonomy over covert operations follows a similar pattern. Early in the Cold War, covert operations were very attractive to presidents. While there was no opportunity for direct electoral gain (as operations were by definition secret), the president was expected to benefit from the more favorable external environment they were meant to produce.[20] This made covert operations, a policy tool subject to very little oversight, a weapon of choice for presidents wary of open confrontation with the USSR (Carson, 2018), mindful of the financial costs of military action (Friedberg, 2000), and sensitive to hypocrisy costs of being seen as violating international law and meddling in the domestic affairs of others (Poznansky, 2020).

2.1 A Conspiracy of Silence

Between 1947 and the mid-1960s, congressional attention to and scrutiny of CIA activities was extremely limited. The structure of the Agency (Zegart, 2000), informational asymmetries between Congress and the Executive, and lack of congressional incentives (Johnson, 2005) made inquiries challenging and rare (Lester, 2015). CIA operations were rarely discussed outside of the Armed Services and Appropriations subcommittees – the two congressional groups that exclusively oversaw intelligence activities. Even within those small secretive groups, debates were often nonexistent, as congressional watchdogs abdicated their responsibility, gave the Agency a wide berth, and repeatedly blocked attempts by the few legislators who deigned to call on the Agency's representatives to account for their finances or activities (Durbin, 2017). Sustained campaigns to increase intelligence oversight were few and far between. Most notable among them were Democratic Senator Michael Mansfield's attempts to establish a Joint Intelligence Committee, modeled after the Joint Committee on Atomic Energy, between 1953 and 1955 (Barrett, 2005, esp. 171–176). Mansfield's resolutions lacked broad support among his colleagues, with the last failing in a vote of twenty-seven to fifty-nine despite a narrow Democratic majority in the Senate. The Eisenhower administration's

---

[20] However, as both (O'Rourke, 2018, esp ch. 4) and Downes (2021) illustrate, even when covert FIRCs succeed in replacing target governments, they often fail to produce improved relations or secure US interests in the long term. Cormac et al. (2022), on the other hand, raises important questions about how to conceive of the success and failure of covert operations, who are the relevant audiences, and how perceptions and narratives can shift over time.

discussion of the dangers of such a committee, however, give critical insight into the political calculations regarding covert operations and congressional oversight. A 1956 memorandum from DCI Allen Dulles, and the Office of the President to the National Security Council regarding Mansfield's proposals for an Oversight Committee on Intelligence is worth quoting at length,

> A basic fact which must be borne in mind in analyzing this problem is that the establishment of a separate congressional Committee whose only functions relate to the conduct of foreign intelligence activities would inevitably mean a closer scrutiny by a much broader membership of the Congress of the activities of the US Government in this field. Although most of the resolutions introduced have referred to "intelligence activities", which might be construed as not relating to operational activities, they all further provide that the DCI is to report to the Committee on "all" activities of the CIA, which makes it likely that any aspect of CIA or related Government operations in this field would come under scrutiny by the Committee.[21]

Dulles went on to describe the risk of increased tensions between the Executive and Congress were such a committee to be established:

> Although it is perhaps not generally understood in the Congress, CIA does not set policy, but carries on its activities only in accordance with policy set by the Department of State, the NSC, and, ultimately, the President. Hence, if operational activities under NSC 5412 become included in the Joint Committee's charter, it is likely the Committee would feel it necessary to know the policy basis for each activity and the State Department and in certain cases the White House itself would become immediately and directly involved, with the resultant danger of incursion into the foreign policy prerogatives of the Executive.[22]

Mansfield would relentlessly continue to push the idea of a joint committee through the 1960s, encountering strong bipartisan opposition each time and rarely being able to bring bills or resolutions to a vote. It would be more than fifteen years before open discussions of more extensive oversight gained traction in Congress, and these calculations continued to color executive decision-making regarding covert operations.

Despite the widespread use of covert action in the early years of the Cold War and the proliferation of spy thrillers in novels, movies, and TV, the CIA's

---

[21] Memorandum to the National Security Council, from the Executive Office of the President. Subject: Proposed Legislation to Establish a Joint Committee on Foreign Intelligence, from DCI Allen Dulles. Pg. 5 January 11, 1956. Eisenhower Presidential Library, Abilene KS.

[22] Memorandum to the National Security Council, from the Executive Office of the President. Subject: Proposed Legislation to Establish a Joint Committee on Foreign Intelligence, from DCI Allen Dulles. Pg. 7 January 11, 1956. Eisenhower Presidential Library, Abilene KS.

activities only became a substantial subject of debate within elite policy circles in the mid-to-late 1960s. We can look to the Council on Foreign Relations' *Foreign Affairs* magazine as a proxy for broader elite attention. *Foreign Affairs* includes articles authored by influential policymakers and academics and was consumed by the same audiences.[23] In the period from 1945 to 1950, there was only one article published that mentioned the CIA; a 1946 article titled "Our Armed Forces: Merger or Coördination?" which focused on post-WWII adaptation and *the need for a* central intelligence agency. From 1951 to 1960 one article was published that mentioned the Agency, but only in passing. From 1961 to 1965, *two* articles mentioned the CIA. The first "Toward a New Diplomacy" (1962), mentions it in the context of foreign policy integration, among a range of other agencies and offices. The second "Slow Down at the Pentagon" (1965), mentions the CIA briefly in the broad context of expanding government bureaucracy. From 1966 to 1970 we see a spike in the number of articles and the extent to which they discuss the agency substantively. This trend would then hit a peak in the 1976 to 1980 period, with a quarter of the articles published in 1978 and 1979 mentioning the Agency, after which these discussions became relatively less frequent but never quite disappeared. Figure 3 plots the number of articles mentioning the CIA each year between 1946 and 1990.[24]

The first article to substantively discuss the CIA, "Intelligence and Foreign Policy: Dilemmas of a Democracy," was published in January of 1969 and is worth quoting at some length. In the article, historian William Brands[25] identified the moment when elites first started to take notice of CIA activities as the downing of Francis Gary Powers' U-2 spy plane in 1960 and the spectacular failure at the Bay of Pigs in 1961. Brands explains, "From then on there were periodic revelations of past U.S. intelligence operations, and after each disclosure there was a new outcry for more control over CIA and less reliance on it." Brands criticized certain alleged CIA activities from 1965 to 1967 and acknowledged that intelligence and covert operations can sometimes conflict with democratic ideals and principles, but rejected the notion that such covert activity should therefore be rejected out of hand. More importantly, he

---

[23] To discern the frequency of discussion relating to the agency, we searched the content of the articles (in the title, text, or references) for any references to the "Central Intelligence Agency" and/or "CIA."

[24] *Foreign Affairs* released four issues annually until 1979 when it began issuing five per year. Despite the additional issues, the number of articles published per year remained consistent – approximately fifty articles were published each year from 1945 through 1990.

[25] A year before the article was published, the author, historian William Brands, spoke at a meeting on the same topic at the Council on Foreign Relations (CFR). CFR meetings, reserved for select members and invitees, closely track contemporary political and policy challenges and are arguably a very good indicator of elite attention.

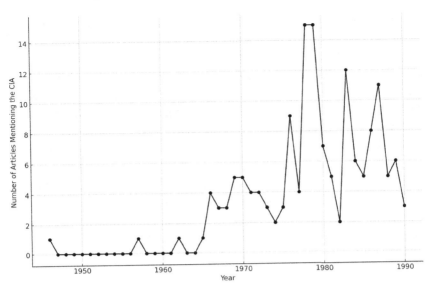

Figure 3 *Foreign Affairs* articles mentioning the CIA.

questioned whether more congressional oversight was likely to improve policy or resolve the inherent dilemma. Rather, he cautioned, that "(a) formal Joint Committee would also create additional pressure on (the) CIA to adopt a cautious and bureaucratic approach in a field where imagination and flexibility are important qualities" and would "reduce the willingness of foreign intelligence services to pass intelligence to, and cooperate with, CIA, because of their fear that such relationships would become known and create domestic political problems" (Brands, 1969, 294–295).

Brands' article is notable because it reflects the old bipartisan elite consensus and marks the point at which it started to visibly erode, nearly a decade after the U-2 incident and Bay of Pigs. The increased attention after each episode was short-lived and failed to generate enthusiasm for oversight. The U-2 hearings in the Foreign Affairs committee were designed less to uncover the causes of the incident or question the CIA's or the administration's management of intelligence-gathering operations and more to discuss potential implications of the event for the Paris Summit and US-USSR relations going forward. The proceedings were kept as distant from the public eye as possible – given the publicity the incident had already received by the USSR and the media – and deliberately avoided discussions about congressional oversight and partisan blame games. In 1960, at a May 26th White House meeting between Eisenhower and congressional leaders from both parties to discuss the incident and the upcoming congressional inquiry, Senator Mansfield asked the president if he would support the creation of a joint committee to oversee the CIA. Eisenhower rejected the proposal emphatically and said that CIA operations were "so delicate and so secret" that he would support "a bipartisan group going down occasionally and receiving reports from the CIA on their activities, but that he would hate to see it formalized." Perhaps more importantly, the president's position was echoed by every other congressman in the room, including the powerful members of Mansfield's own party.[26] Senator Fulbright, who would be heading the hearings in the Senate Foreign Relations Committee, emphasized that he would like to keep the inquiry "on track and not let it stray" and avoid turning the matter into a political one. The only criticism aimed at Eisenhower, by Fulbright himself, was the president's decision to take full responsibility and not disavow the operation.[27] The hearings, initiated the next day, were held in Executive Session (behind closed doors and limiting non-committee members to observer status). As Fulbright promised, the Committee report was only published after White House staff had thoroughly "sanitized" its contents and excluded the entirety of the testimonies by CIA personnel.[28] Hearings following the Bay of Pigs and the Cuban Missile Crisis followed similar dynamics.

It was only the Johnson administration's fateful *overt* military intervention in the Dominican Republic in 1965 that finally prompted Fulbright to question the wisdom of the intelligence and analysis provided by the CIA and to seriously consider the need to establish closer oversight to avoid future unnecessary, costly – the United States lost more than 40 Marines during the botched operation – and damaging interventions. The Dominican fiasco helped push Fulbright, McCarthy, and other Senators in the Foreign Relations committee – mostly Democrats who were already beginning to question American covert and overt involvement in Vietnam – to revisit Mansfield's proposals for a joint committee or perhaps create a new intelligence subcommittee under Fulbright's Foreign Relations Committee. The move, orchestrated largely behind closed doors in meetings of congressional leadership in both parties, provoked fierce opposition not only from the CIA and the White House, but also from senators in the Armed Services and Appropriations subcommittees – especially conservative Democrats and Republicans like Richard Russell and Everett

---

[26] Democratic Senators Carl Hayden, Richard Russell, and Lyndon Johnson (Senate Majority Leader) and Representatives Carl Vinson and Sam Rayburn (Speaker of the House).

[27] Memorandum of conversation, bipartisan leaders breakfast with the President, held in the State dining room, The White House concerning U-2 incident, intelligence and espionage, May 26, 1960. Eisenhower Library. DDE's Papers as President, DDE Diary Series, Box 50, Staff Notes May 1960, NAID 12010079.

[28] The text of the original report is available at United States Congress Senate Committee on Foreign Relations (1960).

Dirksen, who believed that existing instruments were more than sufficient. Mike Mansfield, who had for years pushed tirelessly for a joint committee on intelligence found himself torn between his personal convictions and his new responsibilities as Senate majority leader. He tried to strike a compromise, advocating first the expansion of the existing CIA subcommittees to include members of the Foreign Relations Committee and later the creation of a two-man Foreign Relations subcommittee consisting of the chair and ranking member. Mansfield's main goal in brokering the compromise was to avoid a fight on the floor of Congress. He warned Johnson that a floor debate would hurt the CIA, the Senate, and the White House:

> No party to this dispute will, in any way, shape or form, derive any benefit from this debate except the newspapers and they will, of course, naturally give it the headline-treatment. This will furnish, in turn, further grist for the mill insofar as the C.I.A. is concerned. It will create greater suspicions about it both at home and abroad.[...] creating more and more suspicion and the position of the agency is likely to become much more difficult in the months and years ahead.[29]

Johnson agreed that a floor fight was undesirable, but felt that he could not trust Fulbright, his erstwhile close ally, and other members of his committee not to leak information furnished by the CIA. The president rejected Mansfield's compromise and chose instead to work with Russell and Dirksen to stall and kill the proposals in committee.[30]

2.2 Attention Starts to Mount

Two events in 1967 heralded the shifting grounds. The first was the "Ramparts affair," which CIA director Richard Helms would later identify as the "first sort of unzipping of covert operations that the Agency was involved in."[31] On February 1967, *Ramparts*, a wildly popular left-leaning magazine, published an article documenting CIA involvement with the National Students Association, in supposed violation of the Agency's charter (Hathaway and Smith, 1993; Jeffreys-Jones, 2003; Prados, 2006). The story was picked up by other

---

[29] "Memorandum From Senator Mike Mansfield to President Johnson. Washington, June 6, 1966." FRUS, 1964–1968, Volume XXXIII, Organization and Management of Foreign Policy; United Nations; Document 251.

[30] ibid., document 250 and 259 in that collection; See also "Lyndon B. Johnson and Richard B. Russell Jr. on 2 June 1966," Conversation WH6606-01-10204-10205, Presidential Recordings Digital Edition [Lyndon B. Johnson: The War on Poverty, vol. 2, ed. Guian A. McKee] (Charlottesville: University of Virginia Press, 2014).

[31] Smith, Jack R. "Interview with Richard Helms," 3 June, 1982. CIA FOIA Electronic Reading Room. A Life in Intelligence: The Richard Helms Collection. Document No. 5076de59993247d4d82b5b8e. p.3.

major outlets and led to a cascade of revelations of clandestine involvement with various groups and organizations operating abroad and at home. Criticism came primarily and most vocally from Democrats, with Republicans, including minority leaders, vehemently defending the importance of supporting the cause of freedom by any means necessary. Having learned about the story ahead of time, the Johnson administration was able to anticipate it and enlist support from legislators of both parties, ultimately overwhelming the (primarily co-partisan Democratic) critics at home and counterbalancing the mounting public outcry in foreign capitals. While vigorously defending its actions, the administration also rushed to revise its policy on clandestine funding of voluntary organizations to avoid further embarrassment, but the genie would not go back in the bottle. As Helms later put it, things "settled down again but never to be precisely the same."[32]

The second event in 1967 that proved significant was the creation of the task force that would produce the "Pentagon Papers." Set up inside the Department of Defense to review US military and political involvement in Vietnam from 1945 to 1967,[33] the study would reveal the extent of CIA activities in Indochina. In 1971, MIT researcher and former RAND analyst Daniel Ellsberg leaked the Pentagon Papers to the *New York Times* (Moynihan, 1998; Moran, 2015). The leaked documents, and the extensive coverage they received, opened a veritable floodgate of further leaks, many of which were received and publicized by journalist Jack Anderson, who already figured among Nixon's worst enemies. In the following years, Anderson published secret memos revealing, among other things, US covert support for autocratic Pakistan against democratic India during Bangladesh's War of Independence in 1971[34] and collusion between the CIA and I.T.T. Inc., a Connecticut-based multinational corporation that had allegedly been involved in attempts at subverting democratic elections in Chile against Allende in 1970, and in the United States in 1972.[35] In May 1973, these revelations sparked an investigation by a subcommittee under the Senate Foreign Relations Committee into I.T.T.'s and the Nixon administration's activities in Chile. This "Subcommittee on Multinational Corporations" was chaired by Democratic Idaho Senator, Frank Church.

The Watergate Scandal in 1972–1974 would bring new levels of congressional attention to the president's use and abuse of the CIA and other agencies

---

[32] Smith, Jack R. "Interview with Richard Helms," p. 3.

[33] John Prados (ed.) "Complete Pentagon Papers." NSA Electronic Briefing Book No. 359, NSA, September 6, 2011. www.nsarchive2.gwu.edu/NSAEBB/NSAEBB359/index.htm.

[34] See, for example, Hayes (2012).

[35] The New York Times. 1972. "Anderson Charges 'Plot Against Allende By I.T.T. and C.I.A.," March 21, 1972, Archives.

tasked with foreign and domestic intelligence activities, including surveillance, intimidation, and assassination attempts against political opponents in the United States.[36] Vice President Nelson Rockefeller, Henry Kissinger, James Schlesinger, Phillip Buchen, and James Lynn, in a 1975 memo to President Ford, noted that "[o]ne of the most serious consequences of Watergate was that the intelligence community became a topic for congressional investigation, as well as public and press debate."[37]

In 1972 and 1973, Congress also held various hearings sparked by revelations of secret operations in North Vietnam, as well as Laos and Cambodia during the Vietnam War. Faced with electoral defeat and massive public pressure, Republicans voted in large numbers for the Case-Church Amendment, which officially ended the flow of funds for the war. That same year, James Schlesinger, the new director of the CIA, directed Agency employees to report all activities since the Agency's founding that may be considered *outside the scope established by law*, especially those in the United States. Schlesinger was, above all, determined to get a sense of what other skeletons might be waiting to jump out from the closet and sink the Agency and the administration. The resulting collection of reports came to be known as the "Family Jewels."[38] William Colby, a career intelligence officer and Schlesinger's successor, was intent on keeping the Family Jewels from being publicly released and not having his confirmation hearings become a spectacle. He did not have to try hard; the Democratic leadership in the Armed Services Committees in the Senate[39] and the House[40] were happy to oblige and keep potentially damning CIA activities out of the public eye (Prados, 2003, 262–265). Though Colby's honeymoon with Congress would not last long.

It was under this radical new level of scrutiny that the Nixon administration had to operate when deciding whether, how, and much to support, coordinate, or conspire with Chilean opposition and the military in the Chilean congressional elections in March 1973 and in the lead-up to the September 1973 coup that led to Allende's ouster. As Peter Kornbluh notes, State Department and "senior CIA officials [...] feared the consequences of precipitous military action and believed in the prudence of caution given the ongoing congressional committee

---

[36] The Deep Throat File: FBI Memos Detail Mark Felt's Involvement in Efforts to Identify Secret Watergate Source. DNSA, June 2005, 22.

[37] "Memorandum for President Ford, September 18, 1975." FRUS 1969–1976, Volume XXXVIII, part 2, Organization and Management of Foreign Policy; Public Diplomacy, 1973–1976, Document 48.

[38] Thomas Blanton (ed.) "The CIA's Family Jewels." DNSA Electronic Briefing Book No. 222, NSAs, 26 June 2007.

[39] William Stuart Symington (D-MO), John Cornelius Stennis (D-MS).

[40] Felix Edward Hebert (D-LA), Lucien Nedzi (D-MI).

investigation into ITT."[41] In reviewing continued support for the opposition and the signals that could send of US support for a coup, Acting Assistant Secretary of State for Inter-American Affairs, John H. Crimmins, noted in May 1973 that "[a]nother important factor was the increased sensitivities in the US and in Chile to covert activities of this kind. This sensitivity could well raise the risk level of the enterprise."[42] In a later meeting on June 11, Harry Shlaudeman, the incoming Deputy Assistant Secretary of State for Inter-American Affairs, fresh from his four-year stint as Deputy Chief of Mission in Santiago, noted that "the risk of our assistance becoming known centered here rather than in Chile. […] exposure here would receive a far bigger play and far more credence in Chile than anything that could be said there." The Assistant Secretary of State for Inter-American Affairs, John Kubisch, agreed with his outgoing Deputy, Robert Hurwitch, that "new sensitivities in the US and in Chile to US covert activities should not necessarily drive us to abandon all these, but that they would make it necessary to analyze in a much more critical way than hitherto the importance of the objectives that we were trying to achieve through them," and noted that "in this particular instance he did not believe that the benefits outweighed the potential cost."[43]

A month later, after a failed military coup seemed to imperil the survival of the opposition, Kubisch would become *more* supportive of continued financial support for political parties and private actors opposing Allende, but would again note that "[r]ecent disclosures and allegations about U.S. activities in Chile in 1964 and 1970, together with current developments and attitudes in the U.S. towards covert government activities, make the potential damage to the USG from exposure of this program far greater than in the past."[44] In these debates, as in the cases we will discuss at greater length in the next sections, congressional attention, even absent institutional reform or legislation, directly influenced the perception of political and operational risk and shaped decisions regarding not only *whether* to intervene but *how* and *how much*. A month before

---

[41] Kornbluh, Peter. "CHILE'S COUP at 50. Countdown Toward a Coup" Digital National Security Archive Briefing Book #840, Sep 8, 2023.

[42] "Memorandum From the Director of the Office of Operations Policy, Bureau of Intelligence and Research (Gardner) to the Deputy Director of the Bureau of Intelligence and Research (McAfee)" Washington, May 31, 1973. FRUS, 1969–1976, Volume E–16, Documents on Chile, 1969–1973. Document 135.

[43] "Memorandum From the Director of Operations Policy, Bureau of Intelligence and Research (Gardner) to the Deputy Director for Coordination, Bureau of Intelligence and Research (McAfee)." Washington, June 14, 1973. FRUS, 1969–1976, Volume XXI, Documents on Chile, 1969–1973. Document 329.

[44] "Memorandum From the Assistant Secretary of State for Inter-American Affairs (Kubisch) to the Under Secretary of State for Political Affairs (Porter)"Washington, July 25, 1973. FRUS, 1969–1976, Volume XXI, Documents on Chile, 1969–1973. Document 337.

the coup that brought Pinochet to power, the 40 Committee would approve the continuation of financial support but refrained from expanding the support to new partners in Chile or making more explicit commitments to coup plotters to preserve deniability. In the days after the coup, Kubisch, Shlaudeman, and others would be called upon to testify in front of the House and Senate committees on foreign affairs.

In 1974, Congress passed the Hughes-Ryan Amendment to the Foreign Assistance Act, establishing firmer oversight over covert operations. The vote was close but, importantly, did not fall along partisan lines, in either the House or the Senate.[45] The most important provision in the amendment, which would remain a key focus of contention for decades to come, was the requirement that covert operations were to be reported, "In a timely fashion," not only to the intelligence subcommittees in the Senate and the House Armed Services and Appropriations committees, but to six full committees, before appropriated funds could be spent on these operations.[46] With "timely fashion" left undefined, the main implication of the amendment was to vastly increase the number of legislators who would have access to information related to covert operations – and therefore were able to leak them to the press or disclose them in floor speeches – and could be expected to demand clarification on a regular basis (Durbin, 2017).

As information from the "Family Jewels" was revealed to the public by the *New York Times*' Seymour Hersh, and as revelations about the CIA's involvement in Chile mounted, congressional attention swelled. The straw that broke the camel's back, however, was Hersh's reporting, in December 1974, on the CIA's domestic activities, such as its infiltration of antiwar groups and widespread surveillance of US citizens, including members of Congress. Less than a month after Hersh's first article came out, in January 1975, the Senate impaneled the Select Committee to Study Governmental Operations with Respect to Intelligence Activities, also known as the Church Committee, by a bipartisan vote of 88 to 6.[47] The House created its own Select Committee, led by Otis Pike (D-NY), operating in parallel. The first House Select Committee,

---

[45] "TO PASS H.R. 17234, Rep. Thomas Morgan [D-PA22, 1973-1976] on October 10, 1974, H.R. 17234 (93rd): Foreign Assistance Act." GovTrack. www.govtrack.us/congress/votes/93-1974/h1038.

[46] At the time, the relevant committees were the Armed Services, Foreign Affairs/Relations and Appropriations committees in both chambers. Later, this would also include the House and Senate Intelligence Committees, increasing the number to eight. In 1978 the House Armed Services Committee unilaterally decided it no longer wanted to be notified.

[47] S.Res.21 - Resolved, to Establish a Select Committee of the Senate to Conduct an Investigation and Study of Governmental Operations with Respect to Intelligence Activities. Sen. Pastore, John O. [D-RI] (Introduced 01/21/1975).

chaired by Lucien Nedzi (D-MI), was abolished after the *NYT* revealed that the congressman had been briefed by Colby on the Family Jewels in 1973, prompting members of his own party to question his ability to investigate the Agency. The ensuing battle saw Nedzi reaching across the aisle to sabotage his own committee (Haines, 2004). The Democratic "rebellion" against Nedzi received ample coverage, further fueling public attention.[48] The proceedings and findings from both committees would go on to shine a light on decades of abuses by the CIA, NSA, and FBI and would be highly publicized, making Church and Pike household names and prompting 1975 to be dubbed the "Year of Intelligence."

Throughout, the White House jealously guarded its prerogatives and repeatedly tried to block Congress' access to key information and witnesses on grounds of protecting national security. Gerald Ford came to office in 1974, at the zenith of congressional attempts at clawing back authority over foreign policy. After more than a year of institutional jockeying, in February 1976 Ford issued Executive Order 11905 – reorganizing the intelligence community and issuing a prohibition against assassinations – to ward off further legislative action (Poznansky et al., 2017). As Durbin argues, "While it served to define the organizational and operational boundaries of the various components within the intelligence community, the order was most notable for several provisions that responded directly to the criticisms leveled against the CIA by Congress" (Durbin, 2017, 148). Later that year, the Senate created a Permanent Select Committee on Intelligence, granting it subpoena and investigatory powers to examine intelligence activities, including "covert or clandestine activities affecting the relations of the United States with any foreign government, political group, party, military force, movement or other association."[49] The House followed suit in 1977, creating its own Permanent Select Committee on Intelligence. The votes establishing both committees were bipartisan. In a memo to Brent Scowcroft that spring, NSC staffer John Matheny wrote of the new attention to Agency activity: "Covert action ills are used to justify increased accountability up and down the chain of command – to the point of risking management paralysis by virtue of the vast increase in administrative workload on high-level decision-makers, not to mention increased risks of public disclosure."[50] That summer, DCI George H. W. Bush described his sense of the new oversight initiatives in a letter to Ford,

---

[48] See, for example, Charlton (1975).

[49] "S.Res.400 - A Resolution to Establish a Standing Committee of the Senate on Intelligence Activities, Sen. Ribicoff, Abraham A. [D-CT] (Introduced 03/01/1976)."

[50] "Memorandum From John K. Matheny of the National Security Council Staff to the President's Assistant for National Security Affairs (Scowcroft), Washington, April 24, 1976." FRUS,

The congressional mood towards CIA is improving, but there is still a staff-driven desire to "expose" and to "micro-manage." Staffers demand more and more. Our relationship with the new Senate Intelligence Committee is promising, though their many subcommittees give the appearance of many more investigations. The Staff of the House Appropriations Committee, on the other hand, gives appearances of wanting to run CIA.[51]

As we show later, congressional attention in the 1970s tempered covert FIRCs substantially, though not absolutely or permanently. Covert activities were reignited by shifts in both domestic and international politics in 1979–1980, namely the Iranian Revolution, the Soviet invasion of Afghanistan, and the election of Ronald Reagan. These events put a nail in the coffin of an already-strained détente and reignited demand for US covert operations while also temporarily mitigating institutional battles over foreign policy. Under these geopolitical circumstances and given new authority and responsibility, congressional watchdogs grew weary of overly tying the president's hands. Attention substantially decreased for a spell, and legislators reverted to a more cooperative or delegative stance vis-à-vis intelligence and covert action while still attempting to set some limits. For example, the Intelligence Oversight Act of 1980, which effectively repealed Hughes-Ryan, reduced from eight to two – the Senate and House intelligence committees – the number of committees that needed to be briefed on covert operations.[52] Additionally, it gave the president the option of restricting notification in particularly sensitive cases – as determined by the White House – to only a select few individuals: the chairman and ranking members of each Intelligence Committee and the House and Senate majority and minority leadership, also known as the "Gang of Eight."

The most emblematic case in this period of executive-legislative cooperation over intelligence and covert action was, of course, the "secret" war in Afghanistan, where Congress played a supporting, perhaps even instigating, role. However, as we explain in later sections, throughout the intervention in Afghanistan and the broader "Second Cold War" (Halliday, 1983), policymakers in the Executive continued to worry that increased attention to covert action, even in support of the administration's policies, would limit their options and imperil operations. And while Afghanistan did bridge institutional divides, this truce did not automatically translate to executive control over policy in

---

1969–1976, Volume XXXVIII, Part 2, Organization and Management of Foreign Policy; Public Diplomacy, 1973–1976. Document 74.

[51] "Letter From Director of Central Intelligence Bush to President Ford. Washington, August 3, 1976." FRUS, 1969–1976, Volume XXXVIII, Part 2, Organization and Management of Foreign Policy; Public Diplomacy, 1973–1976. Document 78.

[52] Cutting the Armed Services, Appropriations, and Foreign Relations committees in the House and Senate out of the loop.

other parts of the world. Unhappy with limitations they still saw as excessive, and weary of reporting requirements, the Reagan White House proceeded to authorize new operations with only minimal deference for Congress' formal oversight role while working hard to further "unleash" the CIA (Jeffreys-Jones, 2003, 227). When the White House pushed for authorization to intervene in Central America, Congress pushed back. Reagan moved ahead anyway. In 1982, as the civil wars in Nicaragua, El Salvador, Honduras, and Guatemala raged on, the CIA pursued several operations ultimately curtailed by leaks associated with the Iran–Contra Scandal, where the agency's activities were not only in direct violation of the rules Congress had established but also struck a powerful chord with popular opinion.[53] Congressional attention intensified again, with investigations and hearings dominating the airwaves and the Congress floor during the summer of 1987. The fallout from the investigations dragged on for years, including a spate of indictments of top White House officials well into George H. W. Bush's presidency. The scandal also sparked negotiations between Congress and the White House that ultimately produced the Intelligence Authorization Act of 1991, which introduced a much stricter and clearer set of oversight rules, and which Bush signed despite serious misgivings. We briefly return to how these dynamics have played out in the post–Cold War era in the last section.

3 Measuring Congressional Attention and Effects on Covert FIRCs

In this section, we build on our qualitative discussion from the previous sections and introduce a quantitative measure of congressional attention using content analysis of Congressional Records. Subsequently, we use this measure as our independent variable in a set of analyses where we demonstrate that heightened attention is associated with fewer instances of covert regime change operations. While we go to some length to validate our measure and address possible issues with endogeneity and measurement error with statistical methods, we refrain from making strong causal inferences in this section. In Sections 4 and 5 we provide compelling evidence of how the variation in congressional attention presented in the quantitative analysis causally affected the calculus of decision-makers in the Executive and led to profound changes in not just *whether* (the variation in incidence that we capture in the second part of this section), but also *how, and how much* covert action was utilized throughout the Cold War.

---

[53] "The Iran-Contra Affair 20 Years On." Electronic Briefing Book No. 210, NSA, November 24, 2006.

3.1 Estimating Attention and Its Correlates

We used computer-assisted content analysis of the congressional Record to estimate the amount of attention paid to issues of intelligence and covert activities throughout the Cold War. To start, we built a corpus of approximately 1.8 million speeches made on the floor of Congress between 1945 and 1991 (sessions 79 through 101).[54] The approach we follow is similar to Quinn et al. (2010), but differs in important regards, most notably the fact that we are dealing with a much longer and earlier time period, as well as analyzing both House and Senate speeches. To be sure, using floor speeches to measure attention is not without its complications, especially over such a long time period. For example, it is possible that legislators spent less time discussing intelligence and covert action on the floor of Congress after the creation of additional dedicated committees and subcommittees. If that is the case, our measure might underestimate congressional attention after 1975, leading us to similarly *underestimate* the correlation between congressional attention and covert FIRCs. It is also possible, however, that the existence of specialized committees spurs floor debates on those topics by increasing legislative activity, creating professional and electoral incentives for members to position publicly, and increasing the number of members and congressional staff with experience, expertise, and personal investment in the topic. In fact, Quinn et al. (2010) found that, among Senators, floor speeches are positively correlated with their committee membership. Additionally, floor speeches serve a different, more public function than the work and discussions that happen largely behind closed doors in committees, especially those dealing with national security.

We first identified all speeches that contain words that reference the CIA or intelligence activities.[55] We coded each speech as "1" if it mentions one of the intelligence-related words and "0" otherwise. Using speaker-related information from Gentzkow et al. (2019) as well as additional information on party composition of different branches, we briefly explore the correlates of congressional attention to intelligence as a proportion of all speeches on the floor of Congress. We report some of the results of that analysis here and provide additional historical context to help validate the measure. The historical overview earlier in Section 2 and the qualitative evidence in Sections 4 and 5 provide further evidence that variation in attention cannot be explained by previous covert FIRCs, partisanship, or partisan opposition, or even a single set of laws or

---

[54] The digitized Congressional Records, bound and daily editions, are made available by Gentzkow et al. (2019).

[55] Words and bigrams like "CIA," "Central Intelligence," "intelligence agency(ies)," "intelligence activities," and "intelligence operations."

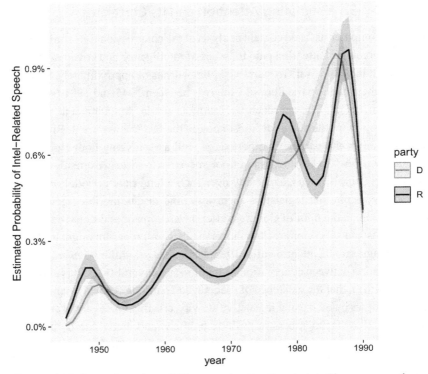

Figure 4 Estimated partisan differences in attention to intelligence over time.

institutional reforms, alleviating concerns with endogeneity, multicollinearity, and (post-)measurement bias in the next section.

Figure 4 plots the results from a semi-parametric model that estimates the probability that any given speech mentions intelligence accounting for the speaker characteristics and allowing for nonlinear interactions between partisanship and time. The two main reasons one could expect temporal variation in the effect of partisanship are, on the one hand, the partisan sorting and realignment that take place during this period, and, on the other, opposition politics, as Democrats might be more likely to call attention to intelligence operations under Republican presidents and vice versa.[56] We find evidence for the former

---

[56] On different dimensions of partisan sorting and realignment since the 1940s, many of which experienced a turning point or accelerated in the 1970s, see Rohde (1991); Clark (2009); Noel (2012); Mason (2015); Lang and Pearson-Merkowitz (2015); Schickler (2016). On how polarization increases the salience of partisan elite cues, see for example Druckman et al. (2013). On the importance of taking these dynamics into account when modeling the effect of domestic politics on foreign policy behavior, see for example Fordham (2002).

and little evidence for the latter. We report the full models and discuss the findings further in Appendix A. While our measure of attention is, in theory, neutral with regard to sentiment or position, the correlations and patterns sketched out here all lend support to our contention, drawn from existing scholarship and confirmed by the actors themselves, that when it comes to intelligence and covert operations *there is no such thing as good publicity*.

Figure 4, as predicted, shows low attention in the first three decades, with a first small bump in attention surrounding the creation and strengthening of the CIA with the 1947 National Security Act and the 1949 Central Intelligence Agency Act. Notably, both acts passed with almost universal bipartisan support. The 1947 act creating the CIA with virtually no congressional oversight authority passed by a voice vote under a Republican-dominated Congress, which Truman nicknamed the "do-nothing Congress" in his re-election campaign. The 1949 CIA Act, which revamped the Agency and gave it access to secret funds for operations, was voted into law by a Democratic-majority Congress, with full Republican support. The only "no" votes in the House were Democrats – and one American Labor Party congressman. The hearings in the Committee on Armed Services illustrate the extent of bipartisan support for the CIA and for keeping its activities shielded from public and broader congressional attention. Chairman Carl Vinson (D-GA) and ranking member Dewey Short (R-MO) agreed that, in Vinson's words, "We cannot have a Central Intelligence Agency if you are going to advertise it and all of its operations from the [...] Empire State Building. So the Congress just has to go along or else not have any confidence in us."[57] The subsequent bumps in attention coincide with Mansfield's failed pushes for congressional oversight and the Bay of Pigs fiasco, respectively. These are followed by a surge of attention in the late 1960s peaking in 1975, appropriately dubbed the "Year of Intelligence," before receding and peaking again in 1987 during the Iran–Contra Scandal. We also find that while congressional attention is on average higher after the reforms of the mid-1970s, there is substantial variation in the periods before and after Hughes-Ryan. We explore the post-1974 variation in greater detail in later sections.

The next step we took to create a measure of congressional attention that we can use to test for constraining effects on presidential behavior was to take all intelligence-related speeches and filter out those speeches that are likely irrelevant to congressional attention to the CIA itself, such as those in which members are merely incidentally referencing intelligence activities in the

---

[57] See House Committee on Armed Services, "Full Committee Hearings on H.R. 1741, H.R. 2546, H.R. 2663," February 23, 1949, page 487.

context of other issues in foreign or domestic affairs. To do so, we extracted these speeches and subjected them to unsupervised topic modeling. We converted the subset of the corpus into a Document-Feature Matrix, from which we removed standard English stopwords, symbols, numbers, and punctuation, as well as words that frequently occur in congressional speeches, but have low information value.[58] Next, we used the R package stm, developed by Roberts et al. (2019), to estimate a series of topic models on just this subset of speeches.[59]

A key challenge in unsupervised topic modeling is selecting the appropriate number of topics, or k. Existing scholarship offers some heuristics and useful diagnostic tools, but ultimately suggests that selecting the "right" k is more art than science. After trying models with between five and thirty topics, we settled on a fairly simple ten-topic model, as this produced topics that are easy to interpret, are readily discernible from each other, score highly on exclusivity and semantic coherence, and produce relatively small residuals.[60] Perhaps more importantly, these various models all identify a single topic that captures speeches relating to congressional oversight of intelligence activities. Figure 5 plots the ten topics, in descending order of prevalence, and the three most distinctive words for each. A cursory glance reveals topics related to energy (10), Soviet nuclear capabilities and strategy (6), international communist subversion (8), and specific interventions like Nicaragua and Vietnam (5). Figure 6 is a word cloud of the 100 most distinctive words to load in Topic 1, the most prevalent topic in the corpus, which we are labeling the "oversight" topic.[61]

3.2 Does Congressional Attention Restrain the Executive?

Having produced a measure that approximates the level of attention paid by legislators to issues relating to the oversight of intelligence and covert activities, we can now test our theory that higher levels of congressional attention can

---

[58] E.g. "senator," "will," "president," "yield," "gentleman," "bill," "vote," "amendment," and "senate."

[59] This is a much more manageable task than attempting to classify all 1.8 million congressional speeches. We also pursued this approach, producing similar but much noisier and less efficient results.

[60] Increasing the number of topics yields only marginally better numbers for "heldout likelihood," residuals, and exclusivity, three common diagnostic values, while sacrificing semantic coherence and human interpretability. If we allowed the *stm* package to determine an optimal number of topics following its built-in algorithm, it produced a 75-topic model that seemed to overfit the data and produce unintelligible results.

[61] This is a mixed-membership model and the same word can be classified as belonging to any number of different topics to different degrees, and accordingly the same speech is classified as being about any number of topics.

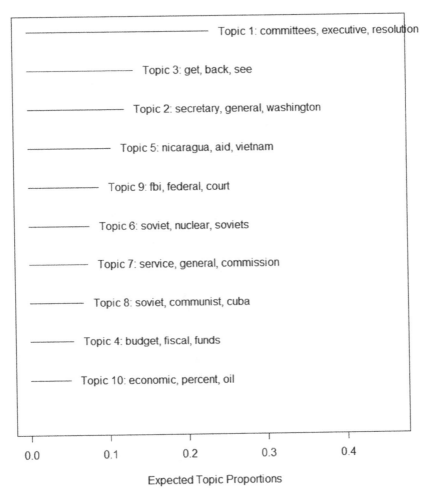

Figure 5 Topic proportions, 10-topic model

constrain the president's use of covert FIRCs. In the remainder of this section, we offer a set of quantitative tests of our main hypothesis that:

- H_1: Increased congressional attention results in fewer covert FIRC operations.

This stands in contrast to other existing domestic-politics explanations of temporal variation in US covert FIRCs. As we suggested in previous sections, these alternative explanations can be summarized as:

- H_{a1}: When the government is divided (different parties control the Executive and Congress), presidents authorize fewer covert FIRCs;
- H_{a2}: Oversight reforms in 1974–75 drastically reduce the incidence of covert interventions henceforth;

Figure 6 Word cloud, oversight topic

as well as a null hypothesis which holds that:

- H_0: Congressional attention and oversight have no meaningful impact on covert interventions.

We draw on two recent studies of US covert regime-change interventions discussed in Section 1 (Downes and O'Rourke, 2016; Smith, 2019). Since we are primarily interested in the effects of domestic political factors on the propensity to engage in these covert interventions abroad, for our main analysis we use the panel data from Downes and O'Rourke, which includes all *known* instances in which the United States initiated covert FIRC operations from 1947 through 1989.

The variables of interest for this portion of the study are as follows:

- **DV**: *Onset* is coded 1 if the US initiates a covert FIRC operation against that country and 0 otherwise.[62]

---

[62] The O'Rourke & Downes dataset includes both overt and covert FIRC operations, but as our theory deals with covert action, we only include the latter in our models.

- **IV**: *Congressional Attention*. We used the estimates from the topic model to produce an indicator of congressional attention to intelligence oversight in a year, calculating the percentage of intelligence-related speeches that relate to oversight. This variable then, is the *estimated percentage of speeches related to intelligence oversight* out of *all* congressional floor speeches in a given year, producing a number between 0 and 1.
- **Domestic controls**: *Divided Government* is coded as 1 if the congressional majority is from a different party than the president's and 0 otherwise. *Election Year* is coded as 1 if it's a presidential election year. *Q1 Approval* is the president's mean approval for the first quarter of a given year.[63] We account for president-fixed effects by including dummies for presidents from Truman to Carter, with Reagan-Bush as the excluded category.[64]
- **Dyadic and Target Controls**: *Relative capabilities* are the target's capabilities (measured by the Correlates of War Composite Index of National Capabilities) as a share of US capabilities. *Democracy* is coded as 1 if the country is a democracy and 0 otherwise. *Active Soviet Operation* is coded as 1 if the country is the target of an ongoing Soviet covert operation according to Berger et al. (2013).
- **Time controls**: *Peace years* is the number of years since the last onset of a US-supported covert FIRC operation in the country, and its squared and cubic terms (Carter and Signorino, 2010).

Figure 7 plots the results from several models.[65] Models 1 through 3 are logistic regressions with robust standard errors. The data for these models are structured as a panel, with the units of analysis being all possible target countries over time. Model 1 includes only *Congressional Attention* and time controls. Model 2 adds the additional domestic control variables described earlier. In all models, *Congressional Attention* is negatively and significantly correlated with the likelihood of covert FIRC onset. The fact that we find consistently negative correlations between congressional attention and covert action onset as our theory predicts also relieves concerns about potential reverse causation. After all, if attention itself were primarily or largely a product of

---

[63] The domestic controls in this section are largely drawn from Smith (2019). See Appendix B for a discussion of corrections we had to make to that data.

[64] In Appendix B, we report results from models not including presidential dummies. Results are largely unchanged.

[65] For a table with the results from each model, see Appendix B. In the graph, to make the visual comparison of coefficients easier, we standardize *Congressional Attention* and *Relative Capabilities*.

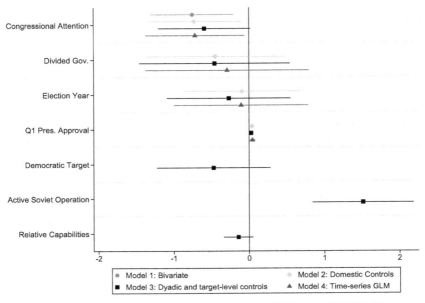

Figure 7 Models of covert FIRC onset, coefficients with 95% CIs

past or current covert FIRC operations, we would see a *positive* relationship in the data. As we suggest in previous sections and reiterate in the cases in the next section, Congress can have their attention drawn to intelligence oversight for various reasons, including particularly spectacular operations, unrelated scandals involving intelligence agencies, and broader battles over foreign policy authority.[66]

Models 1 through 3 do not find statistically significant results for *Divided Government* or other domestic-level controls. This is consistent with Zegart's conclusion that "Divided government does not appear to dramatically increase Congress' incentives or ability to oversee intelligence agencies." (Zegart, 2013, 119)[67] Model 3 adds dyad- and target-level control variables. Among these, only *Soviet Operations* is statistically significant, with the likelihood of US-backed covert FIRCs increasing substantially in countries experiencing Soviet operations. In some models, we find limited evidence for the effect of

---

[66] In Appendix B, we report models using lags and moving averages that should further alleviate any concerns about reverse causation or problematic dynamic relationships.

[67] See Appendix B for details. Smith finds that the effect of *divided government* is conditional on the absence of formal oversight mechanisms. We found, at best, modest statistical support for a conditional relationship, but in the opposite direction.

democracy in the target country and relative capabilities, but those findings are not robust.[68]

Next, in Model 4, we change the estimation technique to deal with a key potential issue with this analysis. Specifically, using panel data with observations at the level of the target country when the variable of interest is measured at the level of the initiator, the United States, might unduly inflate the number of observations without sufficient theoretical justification. In other words, for models without target-level covariates, it makes no difference if the covert operation targets Chile or France. And even the inclusion of those covariates changes little, as the characteristics of any individual country are reasonably exogenous to the changes in US politics.[69] We suggest that a more appropriate analysis may be a time-series analysis, with observations only at the US level and the DV being a count of covert operations initiated in a given year, normalized as a proportion of the number of states in the international system that year. We present these findings in Model 4 in Figure 7. Since this new DV is a proportion, bound between 0 and 1, we can also model it with a Generalized Linear Model in the binomial family and a logit link 7.

We again find that even with a much smaller sample size the coefficient for *Congressional Attention* is still negative and statistically significant ($p < 0.05$), while other domestic-level variables fail to reach significance.

Figure 8 explores the substantive effect of *Congressional Attention* by displaying the predicted probability of onset of a covert FIRC operation (y-axis) conditional on the level of attention (x-axis) from Model 3, with other covariates held at their mean/median values. The effect is not only statistically significant; it is also fairly large. The estimated probability of onset when *Congressional Attention* is at its 90th percentile is less than one-third of the probability when *Congressional Attention* is at its 10th percentile.[70]

In the next two sections, we offer causal process observations from declassified documents pertaining to the attempts to covertly intervene in the civil war in Angola starting in the mid-1970s, as well as additional evidence from later cases. We show direct evidence that heightened congressional attention

---

[68] The finding on democracy, though it may be surprising to some, is consistent with both defenders and critics of US-backed coups as driven by a concern with protecting democracy, or at least what the United States *perceived* as such. See Poznansky (2015); Barkawi (2015).

[69] Clustering the standard errors on the target country may or may not be an appropriate adjustment, depending on the nature of the data-generating or sampling processes, but this is not the case here, as the standard error for the regressor in question is certainly not clustered at the level of the targets. See Abadie et al. (2017).

[70] The difference between the two is statistically significant at $p < 0.05$.

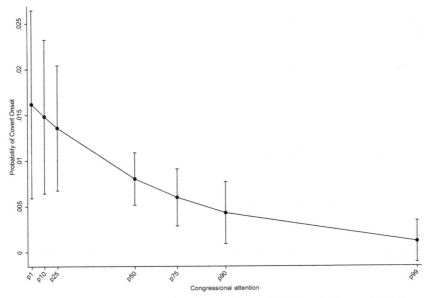

Figure 8 Effect of congressional attention on likelihood of covert FIRC onset, predictive margins with 95% CIs

constrained the president's use of covert FIRCs during the Cold War, affecting where, when, how, and how much covert intervention took place.

4 Hamstrung in Angola and Beyond: Not Just Whether, But How and How Much

In the previous section, we attempted to quantify levels of congressional attention to intelligence and estimate its effect on the likelihood of covert FIRCs. In this section, we offer direct evidence of the causal processes theorized – increased congressional attention changes the Executive's assessment of costs and risks associated with covert operations, thus restraining their use. We examine the case of US intervention against the incipient ruling government in Angola starting in 1974, near the height of congressional attention to the CIA and its covert operations. The causal-process observations from the case – as in the cases that follow – plainly demonstrate that the Executive saw congressional attention to these matters as a real impediment and actively sought to evade or reduce it. This evidence also adds credence to several modeling decisions made in previous sections, such as variable measurement, temporal lags, and periodizations. It also serves to address potential concerns about endogeneity, as the content and timing of the deliberations allow us to clearly see that greater congressional attention had a constraining effect before Angola-specific legislation was introduced and that concerns with further fueling that attention constrained the White House's ability to actively fight to assert its authority on the matter, even after the mood in Congress shifted.

While Angola may appear to be a straightforward "most likely" or "easy" case for our theory, offering relatively little analytical leverage, upon closer inspection, the case proves far more interesting and useful. First, while congressional attention reached theretofore unprecedented levels in the period covered, making this an "extreme case" (Gerring, 2006, 101), existing datasets on FIRCs code this as a case of active intervention starting in 1975, making it more of an "outlier" or "deviant case" (Gerring, 2006, 105) – although we argue the case is a lot less deviant than it appears. Because of this, it is also the most influential case in our regression models, with the largest Pregibon $\Delta\beta$ statistic of any observation, making it an ideal "influential case" to study (Gerring, 2006, 108). Importantly, the case also features distinct change over time in both dependent and independent variables allowing us to identify the effects of *variation* in attention. Finally, while *congressional attention* was very high for much of the period, the 1970s were also marked by unprecedented institutional reforms, divided government, a presidential impeachment, and the start of a significant increase in polarization, realignment, and partisan sorting, all of which would favor alternative explanations as much or perhaps more than our own.[71] Precisely for these reasons, the Angola case allows us to dig deeper into the relationship between attention and covert action as well as potential confounders such as formal oversight legislation, partisanship, and broader structural dynamics, not only evaluating the explanatory power of different variables but also exploring potential interactions between them.

We find concrete process evidence that institutional reforms had a significant effect on covert operations in Angola and elsewhere, but that this effect was *conditional on sustained attention.* The Hughes-Ryan Amendment and Church and Pike Committees were not final watersheds, but discrete moves in a prolonged game of cat and mouse between Congress and the Executive. Limiting legislation itself was unnecessary and insufficient to constrain the Executive, and was only one of several ways in which legislators attempted to rein in covert activities. Echoing Kriner's (2010) research on congressional constraints on overt action, we find that legislative attention affected not only the executive's decision to intervene covertly, but also the duration, scope, and

---

[71] By most measures, absolute levels of polarization and party identification were at their lowest in the 1960s and early 1970s and still low in the mid-1970s – certainly much lower than they would be even ten years later, not to mention today – but the period was a major inflection point, including on foreign policy. See, for example, Weisberg (2002) and (Sinclair, 2014, esp. 115–120). See also footnote 3 in the previous section.

tactics used. Additionally, we find only limited evidence in favor of the partisan dispute thesis, as opposition to Kissinger and Ford's plans for covert intervention in the Angolan conflict came from members of both parties, though it was particularly strong among *liberal* Democrats. Despite increasingly bitter partisan fights elsewhere, White House officials themselves seemed to perceive this as primarily an *institutional*, not partisan, struggle.

The Angolan case also cannot be explained by demand-side perspectives alone. Ford and Kissinger wanted greater covert and overt involvement in Angola to, at first, prevent Agostinho Neto of the People's Movement for the Liberation of Angola (MPLA) from taking power upon Portugal's sudden retreat from the continent following the Carnation Revolution, to push a Jonas Savimbi–Holden Roberto coalition, or at least produce a stalemate that would impede Neto from governing the entire country.[72] Later, the impetus shifted to counteracting Soviet and Cuban intervention in favor of Neto in 1975–77 and preventing the total collapse of UNITA. Despite considerable progress toward détente in Europe in the same period, evidenced by the Strategic Arms Limitation Treaty negotiations, the Helsinki Final Act, and the handshake in space (Ross-Nazzal, 2010), the Cold War continued to rage on in the "Third World," where it was ultimately buried (Painter, 2002, 80–81; Westad et al., 2005). Soviet, Cuban, and Chinese inroads into Southeast Asia, Africa, and Latin America continued to draw ire and concern from American officials. Any explanation of the substantial dip in covert operations during the period, and the relative restraint exercised in Angola in particular, needs to grapple with the constraining role exercised by Congress. US archives relating to the intervention in Angola offer a glimpse into the process by which key officials, Kissinger foremost among them, begrudgingly came to terms with this reality.

During the summer of 1974, the State Department and the CIA, at Ford and Kissinger's request, studied possible courses of action to offer covert financial and military aid to Savimbi and Roberto. Congress was a relatively minor issue at first, as Ford and Kissinger were very confident that the president could make promises and set policy without great concern for congressional approval. However, it became increasingly clear by late 1974 that Congress would now have a significant stake in the process and needed to be brought into the fold. Kissinger exhibited frustration and reluctance at every turn to accept Congress' new role, and more than once attempted to skirt legislative oversight. As the administration struggled to come to terms with the new reality, new covert operations ground to a halt. By January 1975, Kissinger and Ford were both

---

[72] For the effects of the Carnation Revolution on independence movements and civil strife in Lusophone Africa, see Rio Tinto (2017).

ready to support whatever it took to get rid of the requirement to brief six congressional committees – even the possibility of reviving Mansfield's old idea of a Joint Committee, which Ford had fought against as a congressman sitting in the CIA subcommittee of the House Appropriations Committee.[73] The main problem, as far as Kissinger was concerned, was the risk of leaks endangering operatives, creating political scandals, and embarrassing international partners. In a 40 Committee meeting in February, Kissinger said, "He had talked to the President, and we won't authorize any covert operations until we get this straightened out. How can you expect other countries to work with us? Maybe I ought to name an Assistant Secretary of State for Covert Operations since I get blamed for them anyway."[74]

With the war in Angola intensifying and Ford pressing for action, DCI William Colby sounded another cautionary note caution in June 1975: "While it would be useful to give assistance, it would be matched by the Soviets and there could be increased fighting and there would be no happy ending. I don't think we can put up a large enough sum to wrap it up quickly, and, *with CIA's own present exposure*, to get away without a great deal of criticism." When Ford replied that "[w]e can't sit here and worry about six Committees if we do what's right," Colby clarified: "What I'm worried about is *leakage* and *scandal* in the present situation."[75] Weeks later, and still months before Senator John Tunney (D-CA) passed the first appropriations rider prohibiting covert arms transfers or any other paramilitary operations in Angola, when discussing whether and how to assist Savimbi and Roberto against Neto, Colby kept pushing for a minimal footprint in the form of money, without directly supplying weapons or any physical presence: "Let's give dollars and let them decide what to do with it – if they want to buy arms – and this will keep Congress off our backs. [...] Let's go the funding route first. *I'm scared of the Congress on this*."[76] When Kissinger pressed for a larger amount of funds, Colby replied that he "would be wary of trying that now while the House is marking up our budget."[77] Kissinger asked, rhetorically, "How many committees must be briefed?" When Colby responded "six," Kissinger remarked, in deep frustration rather than surprise or disbelief, "Incredible"!

73 "Memorandum of Conversation." Washington, January 23, 1975, 9:35–10:18 a.m. FRUS, 1969–1976, Volume XXXVIII, Part 2, Organization and Management of Foreign Policy; Public Diplomacy, 1973–1976. Document 30.

74 "Memorandum for the Record" Washington, February 1, 1975, 10:30 a.m. FRUS, 1969–1976, Volume XXXVIII, Part 2, Organization and Management of Foreign Policy; Public Diplomacy, 1973–1976. Document 32.

75 "Minutes of a National Security Council Meeting, June 27, 1975." FRUS, 1969–1976, Volume XXVIII, Southern Africa, Document 113. Emphases added.

76 "Memorandum for the Record, Washington, July 14, 1975, 10:30 a.m." FRUS, 1969–1976, Volume XXVIII, Southern Africa. Document 115. Emphasis added.

77 ibid.

In a meeting that September, Kissinger and Colby again articulated the challenge from Congress:

> Colby: We have a problem with Congress and the public.
> Kissinger: But Congress has been informed.
> Colby: Confidentially, but if this was exposed ...
> Kissinger: What does "expose" mean?
> Colby: Publicly – if it became public knowledge that we were sending American arms in.
> Kissinger: And what would that do?
> Colby: There would be a great uproar about CIA getting involved in a war.
> [...] Kissinger: We look like pitiful characters. Angola is about as far away from the Soviets as they can get, so we go to the Chinese who are also about as far away from China as they can get – all because we can't do anything. If this was 1960, you'd win it.
> Colby: Yes, no problem. Because we have to tip-toe through the tulips with Congress – that stops us.[78]

As discussions within the White House and with African partners progressed, it was abundantly clear that Congress was the key obstacle to covert support for Savimbi. As Kissinger noted in a meeting with Ford and Brent Scowcroft, "At the very moment when the Soviets begin to blink, the Congress is going to cut our legs off."[79] The problem was summarized in an NSC meeting the same day by Kissinger and Deputy National Security Advisor William Hyland. Kissinger noted that the administration's leverage in the fight with Congress over Angola was reduced because it was impossible to counter-mobilize the American public without making their strategy and goals explicit and clear – which in turn would fundamentally transform the operation from a poorly kept secret into an outright overt intervention: "It's really something. Nixon went on national television. If the average person doesn't understand what's going on, how can you fight Congress without mobilizing the public."[80] Hyland noted that "...The Senate debate changes things. The only explanation we can make is that we're opposing the Soviets. But it's not clear to the public what we're trying to do."[81] When Kissinger suggested exploiting loopholes in appropriations and just directing funds to hire mercenaries through France and deploy a C-130 transport aircraft to deliver them to Angola, the US Ambassador to

---

[78] "Memorandum for the Record, Washington, September 13, 1975, 9 a.m.." FRUS, 1969–1976, Volume XXVIII, Southern Africa, Document 127.

[79] "Memorandum of Conversation, December 18, 1975." FRUS, 1969–1976, Volume XXVIII, Southern Africa, Document 153. This was two days before the passage of the Tunney-Javits Amendment.

[80] "Memorandum of Conversation, December 18, 1975." FRUS, 1969–1976, Volume XXVIII, Southern Africa, Office of the Historian, Document 152

[81] ibid.

the UNSC (and soon-to-be Assistant Secretary of State for African Affairs), William Schaufele, responded simply: "With the uproar in Congress, I don't think we can do it."[82] As Deputy Secretary of State Robert Ingersoll had put it a week earlier, "Any evidence of a direct approach would be terrible. The political problems are hurting us now."[83]

In subsequent meetings, officials often openly discussed how far they were willing to go in omitting or stretching the truth when briefing Congress. Some, such as deputy to the Assistant Secretary of State for African Affairs Edward Mulcahy, admitted to "fuzzing over" details of US support to Savimbi, while Clements and Colby insisted that they had to "tell them the facts."[84] By June 1976, when the Clark Amendment prohibiting security assistance to Angolan groups without express congressional authorization was signed into law,[85] the impossibility of meaningful support to FNLA and UNITA was already a matter of fact for policymakers, a fact decried often and loudly by Kissinger. In a January 1976 meeting with René Journiac, the special assistant to the French president on African affairs, Kissinger exploded: "This is a national disgrace. The Cubans are able to send 10,000 men to Angola, and we are unable to even send money!"[86] Even in the absence of express prohibitions, having to constantly check with Congress before spending or reallocating money to covert aid in Angola ground US support to nearly a halt, forcing the administration to rely more heavily on US allies, such as Israel, South Africa, Belgium, and France. In the following months, dozens of countries extended formal recognition to Agostinho Neto, what little remained of Holden Roberto's FNLA after the Battle of Quifangondo was decimated, and internal White House discussions increasingly treated Savimbi as a lost cause.

Limited covert support to Savimbi's UNITA continued during the Carter administration, reflecting the president's commitment to countering the growing Cuban presence in Angola, but even the most ardent supporters of increased intervention doubted that anything short of large-scale direct intervention would allow Savimbi to overthrow Neto's MPLA. The only reason to continue supporting the insurgents was to impose costs on the Cubans and Soviets and retain some leverage in negotiations for a political solution to the conflict.

---

[82] ibid.

[83] "Memorandum for the Record, December 11, 1975." FRUS, 1969–1976, Volume XXVIII, Southern Africa, Document 147, Office of the Historian.

[84] ibid. Colby, as head of the CIA, had been the Agency's public face in the Pike and Church committee hearings and was permanently traumatized by the experience.

[85] Section 404(a) of the Arms Export Control Act, 1976

[86] "Memorandum of Conversation," Brussels, January 24, 1976, 7:30 a.m., FRUS, 1969–1976, Volume XXVIII, Southern Africa, Document 172.

In any case, attempts at boosting that support, providing aid directly and indirectly, and encouraging third parties, were severely curtailed if not entirely shot down by actual and expected congressional opposition. The first new operation under Carter was a covert propaganda push to publicize and discredit Cuban forces in Angola. DCI Stansfield Turner, responding to a request from Carter's National Security Adviser Zbigniew Brezsinski, indicated that the Tunney-Javits Amendment, though explicitly aimed only at prohibiting the use of "appropriated funds for our *paramilitary* operations in Angola, is sufficiently ambiguous as to raise questions on whether or not the Agency can conduct *any* covert action in regard to Angola."[87]

In February 1978, a CIA-prepared paper outlined a number of possible measures, ranging from offering more communications equipment to mobilizing broad third-party support and introducing third-party nationals to train and assist UNITA fighters. The paper, having restated the ambiguities regarding the Tunney-Javits Amendment, noted that the first "con" of providing indirect support – before mentioning concerns with horizontal or vertical escalation of the conflict or the effects on US relations with Cuba, the Soviet Union, or other African countries – was this it would "Introduce (the) contentious issue of the interpretation of Tunney-Javits Amendment."[88] A month later, Turner would note that

> More substantial materiel help to UNITA would require consultation within the United States Government *which would be difficult to keep secret*. Compromise of a program of even indirect American materiel aid would work against UNITA […] Our previous covert paramilitary support of UNITA in Angola generated a great deal of controversy. Thus, any new steps which verged on covert paramilitary activities should be considered in the light of the *anticipated* reaction within Congress.[89]

The CIA paper attached to the memo went on to note that "The system of briefing widely in Congress tends to make it difficult to carry out any covert action that does not enjoy virtually unanimous backing in Congress," and that "Angola may be a poor choice as to the place where we try to engage in some further covert paramilitary action. An abortive attempt to reopen the issue of

[87] "Memorandum From Director of Central Intelligence Turner to the President's Assistant for National Security Affairs (Brzezinski)" Washington, June 30, 1977. FRUS, 1977–1980, Volume XVI, Southern Africa Document 7. Emphases added.

[88] "Paper Prepared in the Central Intelligence Agency" Washington, February 17, 1978. FRUS, 1977–1980, Volume XVI, Southern Africa Document 19.

[89] "Memorandum From Director of Central Intelligence Turner to the President's Assistant for National Security Affairs (Brzezinski)." Washington, March 14, 1978. FRUS 1977–1980, Volume XVI, Southern Africa, Document 21. Emphases added.

covert paramilitary support of UNITA – *even indirect – could lead to damage to our capability and flexibility to undertake any covert action in the future.*"[90]

In light of this, Turner suggested that the administration should informally reach out to congressional leaders to assess their willingness to allow for more direct assistance to UNITA, but ultimately any real effort would imply repealing the Clark Amendment, which would require a "major Administration effort [...] with Congress as well as the press and public."[91] As he would find out, even informal consultations with members of Congress presented a liability. Someone in one (or more) of the congressional offices the White House consulted promptly leaked the information to the press, forcing the administration to publicly deny that it was seeking authorization for new covert programs in Angola.[92]

In 1979, Turner prepared another memo advocating for more concrete covert activities to exacerbate tensions between Cuban forces and Angolans and exploit the opportunity provided by Agostinho Neto's death. He noted, however, that these continued to be impossible under the Clark amendment. This prompted a frustrated note from NSC staffer Donald Gregg to Brzezinski expressing that "This issue is a clear illustration of the way in which this country (read Congress), in a burst of moralistic zeal, has hamstrung itself in terms of dealing *quietly and covertly* with a promising situation in Angola."[93] Rather than suggest a frontal battle with Congress, Gregg, having learned his lesson, noted that

> [a]n attempt to repeal the Clark Amendment would most probably become a contentious issue which would draw *attention* to the fact that the United States was trying once again to influence events in Angola. The only hope is that recent developments in and around Cuba may have changed congressional viewpoints sufficiently to allow *quiet* repeal of the Amendment.[94]

Gregg's point is worth stressing: in the realm of intelligence and covert action, publicity is usually the enemy, even when in support of the desired

---

[90] ibid. Emphasis added.

[91] ibid.

[92] "Memorandum From Donald Gregg of the National Security Council Staff to the President's Assistant for National Security Affairs (Brzezinski)." Washington, September 12, 1979. FRUS, 1977–1980, Volume XVI, Southern Africa Document 37; See also Director of Central Intelligence. "Talking Points for President Carter's Meeting with Congressional Leadership about Incursion into Zaire's Shaba Province, Secret Memorandum. June 2, 1978, DNSA collection: CIA Covert Operations: From Carter to Obama, 1977–2010; and (Gleijeses, 2013, 50–54).

[93] "Memorandum From Donald Gregg of the National Security Council Staff to the President's Assistant for National Security Affairs (Brzezinski)." Washington, September 12, 1979. FRUS, 1977–1980, Volume XVI, Southern Africa Document 37. Emphasis ours.

[94] Ibid. Emphases ours.

policy. While Gregg's wish did not come true right away, the environment did change over time as détente continued to falter, and idiosyncratic conditions and political compromises over Africa policy emerged (McFaul, 1989). Despite the changing climate and the weakening of congressional oversight, several attempts to repeal the Clark Amendment were doomed by bipartisan opposition – who usually prevented even putting them to a vote – during both the Carter and Reagan administrations. Prevented from providing direct military assistance to UNITA, both administrations relied heavily on encouraging support from countries such as South Africa, Zaire, and Saudi Arabia while publicly denying doing so.[95] The amendment was finally struck down in 1985. To achieve this, however, the Reagan administration had to abandon all but the pretense of secrecy, retaining only a thin veneer of deniability, and engaging in the kind of public campaign Turner had noted was necessary, but warned against six years earlier.

As noted at the outset of this section, the observed variation in the degree and intensity of US covert involvement in Angola cannot be easily explained by demand or other supply-side accounts and can only be explained in the context of the institutional battles between Congress and the Executive and the various political and operational costs brought about by heightened congressional attention. Although new laws and formalized oversight mechanisms were often instrumental in materializing these costs, they were not themselves necessary or sufficient.

While Kissinger and his peers in later administrations were not reticent to debate foreign policy generally or Africa policy specifically in terms of partisan politics at home, the absence of any references to partisanship when dealing with congressional interference with their designs on Angola is striking. Partisan differences in attitude and behavior, as in the other cases before and after 1974, seem to be driven not by opposition politics, but by ideology.[96] To be sure, the most vocal opponents of the Ford administration's Angola policies were liberal Democrats: Tunney, Clark, and Humphrey. However, Ford also had to contend with liberal Republicans such as Jacob Javits (R-NY) and

---

[95] See Committee on Foreign Affairs House of Representatives (1987).

[96] This finding is consistent with recent work demonstrating that partisan differences cannot fully account for Congress' role in foreign policy (Jeong and Quirk, 2019) and that other variables, including more fundamental ideological or philosophical orientation and individual geostrategic events (Gries, 2020) are important in explaining the different attitudes of elites and the public with regard to foreign policy. Furthermore, while partisan lines have changed over time (Kupchan and Trubowitz, 2007) the president and Congress are perennially motivated by distinct institutional and electoral incentives that may predispose them to cooperation to constrain the executive (Tama, 2024).

Clifford Case (R-NJ), both key figures in the passage of the War Powers Resolution a few years earlier.

In fact, while both the Tunney-Javits and Clark amendments – as well as additional bills limiting aid to Angola – received almost universal support among Democrats, the measures also enjoyed substantial, often majoritarian, support among Republicans. As the case shows, liberal Democratic legislators did not abandon their opposition to covert intervention or unrestrained presidential authority suddenly after Carter's election, nor did conservative Republicans suddenly become staunch proponents of congressional oversight of intelligence operations, in Angola or elsewhere. When, in Carter's last year in office, the breakdown of détente created an opening for the reassertion of presidential authority, the administration found support not only in Democratic hawks like the powerful chairman of the House Foreign Affairs Committee, Clement Zablocki (D-WI), but also Republicans like Robert McClory (R-IL), who made loosening the congressional leash on US intelligence agencies something of a personal crusade. When the Clark Amendment was finally repealed in 1985 by a Republican-controlled Senate and a Democrat-controlled House, nearly one-third of Democrats voted to repeal.

4.1 Attention Fluctuates, Oversight Recedes

These dynamics persisted throughout the Reagan years, in a period of extensive reassertion of executive autonomy over foreign policy and through repeated attempts at circumventing or weakening Congress' foreign policy role not only in Nicaragua but elsewhere around the world. The new administration had decided as early as 1981 that Qaddafi had to be overthrown – it was not a question of *whether* but *how*. Reagan's more hawkish advisors, including William Casey and John Pointdexter, would find that statutes and regulations, especially the Ford and Carter prohibitions on assassinations, were practical impediments to some of their plans, but not necessarily impossible to get around. To do so, however, would require significant effort. Concerns with congressional opposition were partly responsible for repeated decisions not to escalate CIA support of dissidents in Libya, and to equivocate in aiding the abortive coup against Qaddafi in 1984. The Reagan administration also seriously considered a Bay-of-Pigs-style invasion by CIA-supported forces in Chad and Egypt – going as far as writing up the speech to be delivered by the president – but ultimately had to pull the plug on the operation after details of the operation leaked to the press.[97] Some of the internal opposition to these plans came not from

---

[97] Journalistic reports suggest that the operation was also strongly opposed by senior diplomats and the members of the State Department.

those who rejected opposing Qaddafi – the covert intervention to support the anti-Qaddafi rebels in Chad elicited little opposition within the administration or in Congress – but a concern that these attempts at unseating him would result in his death. Reagan administration officials dealt with these concerns not only by insisting that Qaddafi's death was likely unavoidable but not *intentional* policy but also by limiting the direct lethal support for dissidents. During the overt intervention in 1986, when the United States bombed various government buildings, including Qaddafi's primary residence and headquarters, they did so while insisting that the goal was not to kill the Libyan dictator. While it might appear to be an absurd denial of the obvious and there is plenty of evidence to believe that many in the government hoped that Qaddafi would perish in the attack, there is also evidence to suggest that steps that could have been taken covertly to increase the chance of that outcome were not taken due to a fear that details of the attempt would later come to light.[98] Expected congressional opposition also contributed to the reluctance to intervene in Suriname between 1980 and 1987.[99] Reagan considered lending support to a Dutch *overt* intervention in December 1986, but the operation was called off before he could make a decision.[100]

We find similar dynamics at play in Reagan's and Bush's initially timid approach to Panama's Manuel Noriega. Relations with Noriega, a long-term collaborator in CIA anti-communist activities in Central America, deteriorated as revelations mounted about his various extracurricular activities. By the mid-1980s it was clear that he had been feeding false information to the CIA, playing all sides of the conflict, receiving money and weapons from the United States and from Cuba while in bed with drug cartels in Colombia and Central America (Robinson, 1988; Dinges, 1990). While both presidents counted on congressional support in their determination to see Noriega ousted – in the form of condemnations, indictments, and sanctions – both also struggled with congressional opposition to more direct and forceful *covert* efforts to overthrow him. While getting castigated in the public eye for not being forceful enough, senior

---

[98] (Hosmer, 2001, esp. 14–17) There is some debate as to the extent of US covert support, however repeated calls for action by NSC staff and principals suggest that the key policymakers certainly did not believe they were engaged in serious covert attempts to overthrow Qaddafi. Had Qaddafi died in the 1986 raid, Reagan would have likely received an even greater boost in popularity than he did.

[99] Available documentary evidence only shows a dissatisfaction with the military regime and some interest in replacing it, but no actual activities directed at achieving this goal during that period.

[100] See Reagan's diary entries of December 11, 1986 and January 1, 1987. "Diary Entry - 12/11/1986." 12/11/1986. The Ronald Reagan Presidential Foundation; Institute, December 11, 1986; and "Diary Entry - 01/01/1987." The Ronald Reagan Presidential Foundation Institute, January 1, 1987.

White House officials repeatedly traded accusations with leaders of the Senate Select Committee on Intelligence, David L. Boren (D-OK) and William S. Cohen (R-ME). Brent Scowcroft, the president's National Security Advisor, and Dick Cheney, his Secretary of Defense, complained that congressional "micromanagement" of covert operations, restrictive interpretations of rules against assassinations and kidnappings, and demands for real-time updates constrained the Executive's options and ultimately prevented successive covert plans to remove Noriega (Engelberg, 1989; Hoffman and Goshko, 1989).

The institutional impasse was only overcome when, in December 1989, Panama declared a state of war with the United States and Panama Defense Force troops attacked and killed a US soldier stationed in Panama City, providing the Bush administration the excuse it was awaiting to execute an *overt* invasion and extradition. Though the operation was planned in secret without consulting Congress, it involved the extraordinary rendition of Noriega and drew condemnations from the Organization of American States and the UN General Assembly for violating International Law. Nonetheless, congressional opposition was muted and public support was plentiful (Cramer, 2006, 194–196) This case is another useful illustration of how the White House can sometimes tame Congress and wrest control of foreign policy tools if it is free to use the bully pulpit to defend and frame its preferred policies, something it can easily do for *overt*, but not *covert* interventions.[101]

The evidence from these cases also shows that partisan divides regarding covert interventions – as well as overt – grew wider in the 1980s, tracking the growing polarization and ideological sorting in American politics. Even then, though, this continued to be largely secondary to ideological and institutional disputes. The increased partisan polarization of covert action also owed, in part, to the greater attention to the topic itself, which in turn was often driven by leaks and disclosures from members of Congress. Senator David Durenberger, the Republican chairman of the Senate Intelligence committee in 1985, went so far as to say that oversight became a partisan issue when "covert becomes overt."[102]

---

[101] While the bully pulpit is not always an effective instrument and can even backfire, presidents are generally more successful in garnering support and shaping public opinion on matters of foreign policy. In particular, presidents tend to receive public support when they speak publicly in support of military action against dictatorial regimes. As Edwards (2006, 29–34), who is otherwise skeptical of the power of the bully pulpit, notes, Bush's announcement of the Panama invasion was one of only four times he received a substantial approval bump after a major speech. The announcement of Desert Storm was the second. He notes similar patterns for Reagan – Grenada in 1983 and Libya in 1986 – and Clinton – Iraq in 1993 and 1998.

[102] Gertz, Bill. "'Leaky' Oversight Committees Frustrate Foreign Policy Efforts" Washington Times 25 July 1985.

Even in this increasingly polarized environment, bipartisanship and ideological divides continued to trump pure partisanship. While key legislation on Nicaragua was mostly introduced by Democrats such as Tom Harkin and Edward Boland, the first Boland Amendment, amending the FY1983 House Defense Appropriations bill to prohibit aid to rebels with the goal of promoting regime change – and thus precipitating the Iran-Contra scheme – was characteristically opposed by conservative Democrats and supported by then nearly extinct liberal Republicans. The appropriations bill itself was adopted 411–0. A 1983 bill introduced by a Republican congressman to repeal the Boland Amendment failed to even come to a vote, as did Democratic-sponsored bills that would have closed the loopholes in the Boland Amendment and cut off all aid to the Contras. In 1984, after Reagan authorized the mining of Nicaraguan deep-water ports without notifying the Senate Select Committee, it was its Republican chair in the new Republican-majority Senate, Barry Goldwater, who became the public face of congressional condemnation and lent weight to the passage of the second Boland Amendment prohibiting support for all paramilitary operations in Nicaragua, regardless of their stated objective (Mayhew, 2000, 95). Between 1981 and 1983, the Reagan administration dealt with these restrictions in their messaging, both publicly and privately with members of Congress, by denying that the goals of the campaign in Central America included overthrowing the Sandinistas. Rather, they insisted that the goal was primarily to interdict weapons going to El Salvador and Honduras and prevent the spread of violence in the region. Congress' response was to allow aid to be directed *openly* toward interdiction and diplomacy, curbing the administration's ability to use those funds for lethal assistance to the Contras. This policy of denial became harder over time as revelations of the scope of American covert involvement in the region mounted. By 1985, as we noted in the previous section, the "secret" wars in Nicaragua, Afghanistan, and Angola had lost all but the pretense of deniability, and the administration and their supporters in Congress mounted a full-fledged campaign for the authorization of lethal aid to the Contras. In February 1986, Reagan asked Congress for 100 million dollars to be funneled from the Pentagon for overt military assistance, including training and equipment. The House approved the request in March and the Senate in August, clearing the way for a major escalation of direct involvement in the conflict. The vote was split and narrow, but not along clean partisan lines.[103]

---

[103] See Fritz, Sara "Contras Aid Gets Senate Approval: Vote on $100-Million Package Clears Way for CIA to Resume War's Control" LA Times, August 14, 1986.

While the case of Angola illustrates how an attentive Congress can, through formal and informal means, limit the scope and goals of covert operations, other cases of intervention and nonintervention since 1980 further illustrate the continued tensions over executive autonomy and legislative oversight, the substantial variation in attention over time, and the importance placed on avoiding attention to preserve secrecy and deniability. As we will see in the next section, even in the unusual case of Afghanistan, where Congress found itself openly pushing for, not against, intervention, there is clear evidence that the White House, the CIA, and Congress often disagreed bitterly on the appropriate level of congressional involvement, and the risks and benefits of publicity stemming from the attention of Congress.

5 Afghanistan: An Exception That Proves the Rule?

The "secret" war in Afghanistan, arguably the largest covert operation of the Cold War, at a time when congressional attention was relatively high, may strike some readers as disconfirming for our theory. After all, the conventional understanding of the case goes, congressional pressure led to greater, rather than lesser, US involvement.[104] Those familiar with Congressman Charlie Wilson, famously portrayed on the big screen by Tom Hanks, and his outsized role in the CIA's support for Afghan insurgents may be particularly puzzled. In this section, we explain why the Afghanistan case, better understood in its two distinct phases – before and after the Soviet invasion in 1979 – does not contradict our theory, but rather confirms it. A closer examination of the case reveals the constraining effects of Executive–Legislative battles and congressional attention on covert FIRCs, while at the same time calling into question other accounts focusing on partisan politics, formal oversight, or even détente.

As noted earlier, détente was not exactly incompatible with covert interventions. While support for Afghan rebels changed in both quantity and character after the Red Army moved en masse into Kabul, CIA aid for Afghan dissidents against the Soviet-backed regime began well before the Soviet invasion and almost two years before the Carter administration lost faith in détente altogether.[105]

By late 1978, the *mood* in Congress had already started to shift; however, the fact that intelligence and covert action continued to garner so much attention

---

[104] Scholars have found that Congress usually constrains rather than pushes the Executive toward the use of force abroad (Howell and Pevehouse, 2007).

[105] See, for example, "Summary of Conclusions of a Special Coordination Committee Meeting," Washington, June 26, 1979, 9–9:55 a.m. FRUS, 1977–1980, Volume XII, Afghanistan. Document 53. and FRUS, "Report Prepared in the Central Intelligence Agency," Washington, August 22, 1979. FRUS, 1977–1980, Volume XII, Afghanistan. Document 59.

posed political and operational risks that the White House would have rather avoided. In an April 6, 1979, meeting of the Special Coordination Committee, the White House group tasked with evaluating covert operations, members of the committee fretted over how to heed pressures – including from members of the intelligence committees in Congress – to do more in Afghanistan while avoiding exposing American involvement, which the administration had categorically and very publicly denied. David Newsom, Undersecretary of State for Political Affairs, summarized the issue: "If we go ahead with anything that requires a Presidential Finding and reporting to seven committees under Hughes-Ryan procedures, we are running a risk. The American role is likely to come out – knowledge of the American role could change the prospects as far as the Soviets are concerned." Brzezinski replied "That risk is there and its implication is that we should not undertake covert activity at all." The ensuing discussion made it clear that those in the room and their allies in Congress, including the Republican chairman of the Senate Foreign Relations Committee, Charles Percy, understood that "serious covert activities" would require limiting reporting to the two intelligence committees and pressing those committees to "control the leaks." Frank Carlucci, Deputy Director of the CIA, was – correctly – optimistic about the prospect of reform, but cautioned: "That does not meet our immediate problem, however. The law still requires us to brief seven committees." The solution that presented itself was to find a way to delay reporting to Congress until activities were underway, but without violating the letter of the law.[106] More than fifteen years later, reflecting on why covert support was so limited both before and immediately after the Soviet invasion, former DCI Turner explained that,

> The CIA itself was running very scared having had this considerable criticism, and was reluctant, even in the case of Afghanistan after the invasion, to get involved in a major covert activity that might backfire and lead to another Church Committee investigation, and another series of criticisms of the CIA.[107]

The prospect of public criticism continued to haunt the CIA throughout the Reagan administration, ultimately leading to the resignation of Deputy

---

[106] The solution, endorsed by Attorney General Griffin Bell, whose Justice Department had in 1977 issued a secret legal opinion stating that Hughes-Ryan did not necessitate *prior* notice, was to draft a presidential finding but wait to have Carter sign it until after the CIA had received confirmation of Pakistani support, nearly four months after the fact. "Minutes of a Special Coordination Committee Meeting," Washington, April 6, 1979. FRUS, 1977–1980, Volume XII, Afghanistan. Document 48.

[107] "Nobel Symposium 95: The Intervention in Afghanistan and the Fall of Détente, Lysebu, September 17–20, 1995," transcr. by Svetlana Savranskaya, ed. by David A. Welch and Odd Arne Westad. Oslo, Norwegian Nobel Institute, 1996, page 102.

Director John McMahon, who for years resisted pressures for more direct CIA involvement in Afghanistan.[108]

The fact that covert intervention began – however modestly – during the Carter administration and continued at a mild pace at first under Reagan also belies explanations centered on variations in the party in power and opposition politics. Similarly, concerns about horizontal and vertical escalation surely played an important role in keeping US interference limited and secret at first (Carson, 2018), but this apprehension persisted throughout the different phases of the intervention, withstanding profound shifts in US-Soviet bilateral relations. Ultimately, US support reached its highest point precisely at a time when relations with the Soviet Union had begun to thaw following Gorbachev's ascension and outreach.[109]

As discussed, partisan disputes over foreign policy were hardly inconsequential in the Carter and Reagan years, yet here, again, we find, at best, a limited explanatory role for partisanship. Some of Carter's fiercest critics on national security issues, including the anemic response to the USSR's growing involvement in Afghanistan, were hawkish Democrats, most notably Senator Henry "Scoop" Jackson (D-WA).[110] When discussing potential responses to Soviet inroads in Afghanistan, Carter officials noted the importance of limiting Congress' involvement to prevent the undesired publicizing of Soviet activities in a way that could limit the president's freedom of action. In October 1979, Special Adviser on Soviet Affairs Marshall Shulman advised Secretary of State Cyrus Vance that intelligence reports of the evolving situation in Afghanistan ought to be shared with Congress cautiously and selectively. "[A]n intelligence 'breakthrough,' plus a press leak, or a Congressman's statement about 'Soviet brigades in Afghanistan' could put us right back in another US-Soviet confrontation," Shulman noted, adding that Turner should "ensure that intelligence reports on Soviet military actions are not allowed to reach persons who might

---

[108] David B. Ottaway and Patrick E. Tyler. "CIA Deputy Chief McMahon Resigns," *Washington Post*, March 5, 1986.

[109] The US supply of Stinger missiles and other weapons was a topic of open conversation and regular friction in talks between American and Soviet officials after 1986 as they tried to coordinate a de-escalation of the Cold War and, after 1988, a political solution to the conflict in Afghanistan. See, for example, "Memorandum of Conversation," Moscow, April 14, 1987, 9:35–11:55 p.m. FRUS, 1981–1988, Volume VI, Soviet Union, October 1986–January 1989. Document 44; Digital National Security Archive, "Memorandum of Conversation: Special Working Group on Afghanistan," March 22, 1988.

[110] The second iteration of the famed "Committee on the Present Danger," whose mission was to lobby for a more "muscular" policy vis-à-vis the USSR, included prominent conservative Democratic national security voices like Paul Nitze and Maxwell Taylor, as well as prominent members of the centrist Coalition for a Democratic Majority.

make them public in a sensational manner."[111] The putative Congressman in Shulman's admonition was not one of the president's Republican opponents like Strom Thurmond (R-SC) or Barry Goldwater, but Frank Church, Carter's staunch ally in the Senate. A month earlier, Church had dealt a deadly blow to SALT II, the arms limitation treaty that became synonymous with détente, when he made a public statement on the campaign trail breaking the news of a "Soviet brigade in Cuba," demanded its withdrawal, and effectively tied the removal to the passage of SALT in the Senate.[112] Here, reporting requirements and formal oversight mechanisms, and heightened attention together had the potential to force the administration to adopt a prematurely aggressive posture which might have, paradoxically, complicated ongoing covert operations as well as other foreign policy priorities.

The Red Army airlift into Kabul on December 24, 1979, changed the situation dramatically in ways that complicate comparisons with other cases. First and foremost, it meant that the rebels were no longer fighting simply to overthrow a foreign-backed regime but rather resisting a foreign occupying power directly. The change in the nature of the case, from covert FIRC to a full-blown proxy war against a nuclear-armed superpower, would lead us to expect somewhat different processes and outcomes. While the invasion provided justification for a greater level of covert support, including material support, for Afghan rebels, whatever little hope existed of success through covert means vanished quickly, and the focus shifted toward overt diplomatic, economic, and even military measures. While we could then reasonably dispense with the Afghan case from 1980 on for falling somewhat outside the scope of our theory, it is useful to note that even in that new phase of the conflict elements of our theory were still at play, suggesting that the theory has broader explanatory power, while other supply-side theories focusing on partisan opposition and formal institutions may have limited purchase.

Covert support for insurgents grew after the invasion,[113] but had to be re-evaluated and placed in the context of a larger coordinated response. US

---

[111] "Memorandum from the Secretary of State's Special Adviser on Soviet Affairs (Shulman) to Secretary of State Vance." Washington, Oct 3, 1979, FRUS, 1977–1980, Volume XII, Afghanistan. Document 70.

[112] On Church's motivations, see for example (Hampson, 1984, 158–159). Church was joined in his demands by fellow Democrats, like Senator Richard Stone (D-FL), as well as many Republicans, including presidential hopeful Ronald Reagan. The problem, as later became clear, was that Soviet forces in Cuba were not the result of a build-up on the island, but skeletal remains of the force established in the 1960s and never fully withdrawn, meaning that the crisis had been entirely an artifact of increased surveillance of activities on the island.

[113] See, for example, "Memorandum From Director of Central Intelligence Turner to the Deputy Director of Central Intelligence (Carlucci) and the Deputy Director for Operations (McMahon)," Washington, January 18, 1980, FRUS, 1977–1980, Volume XII, Afghanistan, Document 173.

National Security Council officials occasionally suggested in the following weeks that the invasion might create an opening to remove congressional obstacles to covert operations, not primarily in Afghanistan itself but in other parts of the Third World. They predicted, perhaps too optimistically, that congressional and public support for assisting Afghan rebels and making a big public display of resolve against Soviet aggression would be forthcoming. At that moment, the main impetus for keeping that assistance limited and secret, and operating through proxies such as Pakistan, China, and Saudi Arabia, was not necessarily avoiding public condemnation, but avoiding escalation (Carson, 2018). Consequently, the main battle with Congress pertained to the authorization of military and economic aid to Pakistan, which had been all but terminated by the Glenn (D-OH) and Symington (D-MO) amendments to the Foreign Assistance Act of 1961, following revelations of Pakistan's suspect nuclear activities in the mid-1970s. Carter failed to secure support from either Republicans or Democrats.[114]

As the war dragged on and insurgents showed themselves capable and committed to attriting the Soviet occupation, material support became increasingly important. It also became harder and harder to keep the intervention secret. Despite growing pressure from Cold War hawks; civil society groups like the Committee for a Free Afghanistan and the Afghanistan Relief Committee; and numerous media reports revealing aspects of the secret aid to the Mujahideen, the Reagan administration insisted on routing support through allies and partners and keeping a veneer of plausible deniability. Justifications for avoiding direct involvement, particularly in the form of supplying US-made weapons, ranged from fears of horizontal escalation into Pakistan and tit-for-tat responses in Central America to concerns about limited supplies and ability to control where the weapons would end up, to considerations of potential political costs from publicity, referring to the scandals of the 1970s (Kuperman, 1999).

The Congressman most often associated with support for the Mujahideen, Charles Wilson, was a liberal Democrat from Texas. Not only was his intense interest in the Afghan resistance idiosyncratic and at odds with his party's public stance on Reagan's covert wars, he exercised his outsize influence not through legal and formal instruments of congressional oversight, but through informal – perhaps unconstitutional – means. Unhappy with the lack of support the Afghan rebels were getting in Washington, but understanding the importance of secrecy for the success and sustainability of the intervention, Wilson's main contributions to the early effort were not in pressuring the administration in the media, grandstanding on the floor of the Congress, or other

---

[114] Glenn would continue to vocally oppose aid to Pakistan despite his avowed support for Afghan rebels well into the end of the conflict. See, for example, Crawford (1987).

such public acts. Rather, he yielded his influence by forging back-channels with domestic and foreign partners and abused his position in the House Defense Appropriations Subcommittee to channel funds to secret programs he felt were insufficiently resourced, often skirting the jurisdiction of the House and Senate Intelligence committees (Crile, 2003). The result was that he often managed to boost support for the Mujaheddin while making friends across the aisle in the Executive branch.

Other members of Congress in both parties chose a more public route to shake Reagan from his hesitation and had correspondingly mixed results. In 1984, Paul Tsongas (D-MA) and Don Ritter (R-PA) introduced a resolution demanding "material assistance" to be supplied to the Afghan rebels. The resolution was co-sponsored by seventy-five members of both parties and was passed as a Concurrent Resolution with unanimous support in the Senate and an affirmative voice vote in the House. Before the resolution was put to a vote, however, "the State Department and CIA lobbied vigorously in opposition, watering it down to a more ambiguous call to 'support effectively' the rebels" (Kuperman, 1999, 225). Public calls for more robust aid to Afghan rebels became increasingly frequent, attracting Democratic and Republican champions in a split Congress (Republican-majority Senate and Democratic-majority House). In 1985, members of both parties formed the Congressional Task Force on Afghanistan, holding public and private hearings. Senators and Representatives traveled to Pakistan to meet with Afghan rebels and cheer on the brave "freedom fighters." In 1986 Reagan finally authorized the provision of the now-famed Stinger anti-aircraft systems, as well as other US- and UK-made weapons. While congressional and advocacy-group pressure may have played a role in Reagan's decision, others have noted that the policy shift was driven more by changing assessments of the likelihood of victory and the risk of escalation, as well as the lobbying efforts of key officials within the administration, including Bill Casey at the CIA and Fred Iklé and Michael Pillsbury at the DoD (Kuperman, 1999; Heymann, 2008).

After the last Red Army divisions left Afghanistan, the Reagan – and later Bush – administration, buoyed by optimistic assessments of imminent regime collapse, continued to press for a victory of the US-backed rebels against the Soviet-backed Afghan government, even as they outwardly sought a negotiated solution in dialogues with the Soviet Union.[115] The operation had once

---

[115] See, for example, the first National Security Directive of the Bush administration on Afghanistan. Digital National Security Archive. "National Security Directive 3. Subject: U.S. Policy Toward Afghanistan, February 13, 1989." Available at: https://nsarchive.gwu.edu/document/18263-national-security-archive-doc-15-national.

again become one aimed at regime change, but it was only partly covert. Elements of US support remained secret and the White House continued to buck congressional oversight, but US involvement was well understood and often discussed in open channels with the USSR. As neither a peace settlement nor a rebel victory proved imminent,[116] scrutiny of US support for the Mujahideen increasingly focused on the threat of "radical groups" with advanced American weaponry (Goldman, 1992). The Stinger, to this day considered – rightly or wrongly[117] – a game-changer for the Afghan resistance, also became a focus of criticism when it began to pop up in the black market and other conflict zones. The mood in Congress began to turn sour and a debate emerged between die-hard supporters and critics, who believed that with the Soviet occupation over there was no overriding justification for continuing involvement in a civil war in a faraway land, especially if American involvement seemed to be contributing to the undue prolongation of the fighting. Congresspeople, especially Democrats more broadly critical of the administration, pushed for major changes in how the White House pursued its Afghanistan policy.[118] Even longtime supporters like Wilson himself came to view a political settlement of the conflict as an acceptable conclusion.

To be sure, mounting pressures in Congress and fissures in the conservative coalition were only one of several factors that drove the Bush administration to roll back its support for the Afghan insurgents, but likely an important factor, as the president would have preferred to save his political capital for fighting more important battles. At the time of writing, most of the relevant archival evidence remains classified or is undergoing review for declassification. Future scholars will be better able to evaluate the extent to which political costs played a role in the president's decision.

6 Conclusion

We have argued that congressional attention increases the political costs for the president to authorize covert action to weaken and topple foreign

---

[116] The Najibullah government outlived the Soviet Union itself by four months.

[117] Evidence from Soviet archives and critical oral histories with Soviet officials strongly suggest that Gorbachev had decided to end the war before the Stingers started to be delivered. See, for example, Christian Osterman, "New evidence on the war in Afghanistan" Cold War International History Project Bulletin, Issue 14/15; Kuperman. Stingers; Nobel Symposium 95: The Intervention in Afghanistan …

[118] See for example, Representative Lee Hamilton (D-IN) pointedly questioning Assistant Secretary of State John Kelly on the need to maintain the policy of secretly aiding the Mujaheddin rather than making policy more transparently and democratically. See United States Policy Toward Afghanistan. Hearing Before the subcommittees on Europe and the Middle East and Asian and Pacific Affairs of the Committee on Foreign Affairs, House of Representatives, One Hundred and First Congress, Second Session, March 7, 1990, page 35.

governments. We found evidence of this relationship through content analysis of Congressional Records, statistical analysis of covert regime change operations during the Cold War, and causal-process observations of executive decision-making in several key Cold War cases.

We also demonstrated that legislative reforms and divided government were insufficient to affect the president's calculus regarding covert operations, nor were they strictly necessary to restrain the Executive. Laws and formal oversight mechanisms can empower Congress, but legislators must be attentive and willing to wield that power. Presidents' motivations and preferences, while generally relevant in explaining decisions related to foreign interventions (Saunders, 2009), also fail to account for the variation we observe.

One alternative explanation alluded to but not tested in the preceding analysis concerns the role of public opinion in curtailing covert FIRCs. Rather than suggest that public opinion never enters the calculation, we find, like most scholars of foreign policy, that public opinion's role is at best heavily conditioned by that of elites.[119] We do not find that decision-makers generally viewed public opinion as an independent constraint on covert action. Rather than this indicating a disregard for the opinions of average Americans, this omission might suggest a *more sophisticated* understanding of public preferences and attention than usually assumed.

Chicago Council Surveys conducted in December 1974, at the height of controversies surrounding the CIA, found a rather split and somewhat apathetic public. Using a large stratified national sample, the survey asked whether secret political operations should be cut back or kept the same. 7.2% responded they should be expanded, 39.19% said they should be cut back, 27.36% wanted them kept the same, and 25.84% were "not sure" (.04% not ascertained) (Rielly, 1975, 71–73). Greater proportions of respondents favored cutting back "economic aid to other countries" (55%), "military aid to other countries" (70%), and "defense spending" (42%). When asked if they felt the CIA should be more important, less important, or about the same, 14.35% responded "more important," 27.06% "less important," 34.33% "about as important," and 22.07% "not sure" (2.05% not ascertained) (Rielly, 1975, 81). When asked how they would rate the job the CIA is doing as the government's chief foreign intelligence agency, 4.89% replied "excellent," 25.91% "pretty good," 24.38% only "fair," 14.14% "poor," and 29.81% "not sure" (0.86% not ascertained) (Rielly, 1975, 140). When asked if they believed "… the CIA should or should not work inside

---

[119] For a broader discussion of the effects of public opinion on US foreign policy see Holsti (2004, 1992); Risse-Kappen (1991); Almond (1956); Lippmann (1946); Wittkopf (1990); Page and Shapiro (2010); Tama (2024).

other countries to try to strengthen those elements that serve the interests of the United States and to weaken those forces that work against the interests of the United States?" 42.46% replied "should," 25.85% "should not," and 30.2% "not sure" (1.189% not ascertained) (Rielly, 1975, 141). It is striking that in all questions the majority replied either positively, neutrally, or that they did not know. Although it is possible that a small vocal minority was pushing congressional action on covert action, there is little evidence to support this. While Congress often utilized publicity surrounding leaks (many of which were initiated by legislators themselves) as leverage to probe the Executive's use of covert instruments, public opinion seemed to have had little to no independent effect. Furthermore, as we demonstrated in previous sections, increases in congressional attention often preceded and outlasted public scandals.

Although we did not deal extensively with the "demand-side" or target-specific explanations of covert action, we find that our theory complements rather than contradicts much of that scholarship. Our findings have important implications for that body of work, as legislative constraints affect presidents' ability and willingness to respond to increased demands for covert intervention in any particular case. We see, for example, that congressional attention continued to play a limiting role in US covert actions after the demise of détente, moderating the scale and types of covert intervention in the latter stages of the Cold War.

Relatedly, a closer look at the qualitative evidence suggests that existing datasets are not granular enough to capture the full extent of variation in covert action and the wide-ranging effects of Executive-Legislative battles on presidents' freedom of movement and how covert means are employed to achieve objectives. Even when congressional attention was insufficient to forestall or abort covert regime-change interventions entirely, it still greatly affected timing, tactics, and the extent of direct US involvement, affecting the likely outcomes of those interventions. Future extensions and refinements of existing data sets should consider moving beyond dichotomous or categorical measures to allow for more granular quantitative tests.

While we suggested some potential drivers of congressional attention here, future quantitative or multi-method research can more thoroughly investigate why and when legislators tune in and speak up on the issue. Cultural shifts, leaks of sensitive information,[120] reports that expose executive overreach in

---

[120] Evidence suggests that the relevant leaks were symptomatic of the increased attention, largely coming from dissatisfied elites. See also Franck and Weisband (1979) and Kriner (2010). Similarly, scholars have argued that the media plays largely a supporting role, primarily following elite cues, rather than leading independently (Howell and Pevehouse, 2007).

other areas, the relationship between Congress and the media more broadly, and the effects of both successes *and* failures in intelligence in precipitating attention should prove areas of particular interest.[121] Similarly, scholars could also explore how and how effectively actors within the target state or in other countries drew attention to successful *and* unsuccessful US covert regime change operations, and how this, in turn, contributed to increased constraints on US foreign policy.

Another area of future inquiry would be to investigate how leaders conceptualized the trade-offs of covert foreign-imposed regime change operations with regard to international audiences. For example, how did the White House consider relationships with partners and allies or their standing in international bodies when considering authorization of an operation or how the operation would be conducted? Evidence from the cases we analyzed suggests that American officials often worried not only about how disclosures would endanger or embarrass the United States and its agents but also how it would affect foreign partners and therefore the ability to secure their cooperation.

Scholars can also examine how congressional attention and corresponding executive constraints affected other intelligence activities. In particular, as this dynamic affects the frequency of operations and corresponding tactics, duration, and timing, future research can examine if and how the Central Intelligence Agency adapted human and signal intelligence collection activities to preempt further scrutiny. Similarly, others might study how increased attention affected the policies and practices of other intelligence services, such as the Bureau of Intelligence and Research, the National Security Agency, and Military Intelligence. Was this associated with reforms in practice that, cumulatively, led to observable changes in US foreign policy?

Though exploring these dynamics in the post–Cold War and post-9/11 periods is outside the scope of this Element, it is also worth reflecting on how the factors that shaped policy-making during the Cold War might continue to inform policy today. This is particularly important when considering the contemporary *policy* implications of our findings. An analysis of post–Cold War data on congressional speeches would likely find a more significant correlation between partisanship and attention to intelligence oversight, and more polarization in the positions, than the one we find in our Cold War sample. This would be in line with our quantitative (Section 3 and models and discussion in Appendix A) and qualitative (Sections 3, 4, and 5) findings. The evidence we present indicates that partisan differences were relatively small and secondary throughout the period, but they became more pronounced in the late

---

[121] For rich qualitative accounts, see for example Lester (2015); Snider (2015).

1970s and especially in the mid-1980s. Much of this growing difference was driven by ideology and partisan sorting along lines of ideology and/or orientation (liberal/conservative, interventionist/noninterventionist), *aside from and in addition to* the much nastier dynamics of partisan warfare that have received so much attention. While we find some evidence for the latter even in the 1980s, we would expect pure opposition politics – or what Lee (2009, 2016) calls partisan "teamsmanship" or "bickering" – party discipline, and obstructionism to be more substantial factors after the political emergence of Newt Gingrich and into the 2000s.[122] That said, even in these bitterly polarized times, we expect to find that partisanship and opposition politics are still insufficient to fully explain congressional interest in and ability to constrain the president's use of covert action. Additionally, we would expect that the informal mechanisms prevalent in earlier times would be all the more important today when meaningful institutional reform and legislation are difficult to achieve.

In that sense, our study generates expectations that are congruent with recent scholarship that finds that though partisan polarization has arguably reached new heights in the last two decades, bipartisanship is still *relatively* common on matters of foreign policy (Tama, 2024). Recent studies have also shown that Congress' role in intelligence oversight, in particular, has not been immune to polarization and partisan warfare, but neither has it become dominated by these dynamics (Zegart, 2013; Boucher and Gagnon, 2024). In examining the investigation into Russian ties to the 2016 Donald Trump campaign, Kriner and Schickler argue that "[t]he sprawling, high-profile investigation into the Trump campaign's relationship with Russia cuts against the assumption that significant congressional oversight of the executive branch is confined to periods of divided party control"(Kriner and Schickler, 2018, 436). This does not mean that politics stops at the water's edge in the 21st century any more than it did in the twentieth, but rather that just as it did then, politics now is not only about partisanship. Ideology, the inherent relationship between covert operations and issues of human and civil rights, and institutional jockeying continue to play a powerful role in explaining the positions that legislators take on key issues relating to covert and clandestine operations.

Ten years after the 1991 Intelligence Authorization Act was adopted, the attacks on September 11 substantially increased deference to the executive on foreign policy. This was reflected in the largely bipartisan support for both the Patriot Act and the Authorization to Use Military Force Against Iraq in 2002 (Kupchan and Trubowitz, 2007; Snyder et al., 2009). It will be years until

---

[122] For evidence of similar patterns in the politics of foreign policy in other issue areas, see for example DeLaet and Scott (2006).

official records documenting the decisions surrounding the secret wars waged, not only in Iraq and Afghanistan, but also the broader Middle East and beyond, are declassified. At first glance, however, it seems the push and pull between the White House and Congress on intelligence and covert action oversight has continued into the post–Cold War years, and that many of the patterns we identified in our analysis are still visible today. We see them at play in the massive intelligence overhaul of 2003–2004, debates about implementing the 9/11 Commission recommendations, and battles over "enhanced interrogation" and notification requirements for covert operations. Republican control of the House, Senate, and White House cannot account for how much Democrats went along with delegating authority to the president and abdicating oversight responsibilities. But neither can it account for bipartisan Republican-led efforts to oppose certain administration policies (e.g. John McCain's Detainee Treatment Act).[123]

Partisan opposition politics also fails to account for the fact that Democrats not only pushed harder for intelligence oversight after they gained control of Congress in the last years of the Bush administration, but that they also continued to do so under Obama, clashing with the new administration over the Intelligence Authorization Act of FY2010 and, in particular, the provisions that expanded the White House's obligations to notify congressional committees of covert operations. Democrats, led by Senate Select Intelligence Committee Chairwoman – and historically staunch CIA supporter – Dianne Feinstein, tried to increase the number of members of Congress who would have access to that information and to assert the committees' authority to determine the scope and requirements for those notifications. The Obama White House, in turn, went so far as to threaten to veto the bill.[124] Feinstein captured headlines again four years later when she "reluctantly" took to the floor of Congress to reveal details from a classified, redacted report the Committee had produced and accuse the CIA of deliberately destroying and withholding evidence from her committee's investigation into the Agency's past torture activities. The move, she argued, was a deliberate and necessary one, in light not only of the White House's opposition to releasing the full report but also as a reaction to the CIA's reported use of surveillance and intimidation of Senate staff.[125]

---

[123] See for example, Shane, Scott. 2008. "Congress Presses Interrogation Issue with Administration Officials." The New York Times, June 11, 2008; "Bush Accepts Sen. McCain's Torture Policy." NBC News. December 15, 2005.

[124] The bill would have ended the Gang of Eight but did not go as far as the seven or eight committees during the Hughes-Ryan era. See Cumming (2011, 11).

[125] Dan Roberts and Spencer Ackerman, "Feinstein accuses CIA of 'intimidating' Senate staff over torture report" The Guardian, Washington, Tue, March 11, 2014; Baker, Peter. Bruck, Connie. "Dianne Feinstein vs. the C.I.A." The New Yorker, June 15, 2015. "A Prime Legacy

Declining support for the wars in Afghanistan and Iraq sapped confidence in the Executive and likely created an environment more conducive to a string of high-profile leaks, including the leaks from Wikileaks in 2010 and Edward Snowden in 2013. Unlike in the 1960s and 1970s, the initial bipartisan response to the revelation of abuses of executive authority abroad was an overwhelming condemnation of the leakers/whistleblowers and a defense of the government's right to secrecy, except for a few voices on the progressive and libertarian left and a few more among the libertarian right.[126]

In both cases, the limited criticism aimed at the Pentagon, White House, CIA, and NSA among political elites in Congress and beyond was focused on the violations of privacy and civil rights of American citizens targeted for assassinations or surveillance, or the timid response to the leaks. In both cases, Republican criticism of the Obama administration eventually caught up with the denunciations of Julian Assange, Chelsea Manning, and Snowden, but centered not on abuses committed by the administration, but rather its failure to prevent the leaks and the resulting blow to American reputation and power.[127] In 2013, after the initial rash of condemnations against Snowden (and Glenn Greenwald and others who published the leaked material) passed, the first voices to call for increased oversight in the wake of the NSA surveillance scandal came from Obama's own party, with the help of Ron Paul libertarians and Tea Party Republicans.[128] The resulting legislation

---

for Feinstein: The Torture Report on Terrorism Suspects." The New York Times, September 29, 2023.

[126] On elite reactions to Snowden, see for example Burns, Alexander. "Establishment Harsh on Snowden." POLITICO, June 12, 2013. Public opinion at the time was far more divided – though not along partisan lines – and less clear on their opinion of Wikileaks and Snowden's actions. On public opinion regarding Wikileaks, showing that Republicans were somewhat more likely to view them as damaging to US interests and standing, see Pew Research Center. "Most Say WikiLeaks Release Harms Public Interest," December 8, 2010. On mixed reactions to Snowden, see "More Americans Oppose Edward Snowden's Actions Than Support Them," NBC News. June 1, 2014; "U.S. Voters Say Snowden Is Whistle-Blower, Not Traitor, Quinnipiac University National Poll Finds; Big Shift On Civil Liberties vs. Counter-Terrorism | Quinnipiac University Poll," July 10, 2013; Pew Research Center. "Public Split over Impact of NSA Leak, But Most Want Snowden Prosecuted," June 17, 2013. See also Touchton et al. (2020) for a more systematic analysis of public opinion.

[127] See "Republicans Slam White House over WikiLeaks Response." CNET, Nov 30, 2010; Zengerle, Patricia, and Rachelle Younglai. "Republicans Blast Obama over Snowden as Case Turns Partisan." Reuters, June 25, 2013. External observers, meanwhile, including US allies and partners, tended to focus on the revelations themselves and viewed elite reactions as excessive and somewhat hypocritical. See Erlanger, Steven. "Europeans Criticize Fierce U.S. Response to Leaks." The New York Times, December 9, 2010.

[128] Notably John Conyers (D-MI) Rand Paul (R-KY) and Justin Amash (R-MI). Ron Paul himself praised Snowden's "great service to the country." See Weigel, David. "Congress Reacts to Obama's NSA Speech; Or, How Obama Didn't Convince Anybody." Slate, January 17, 2014.

and reforms strengthening oversight and ending parts of the surveillance programs that targeted Americans did little to curb surveillance of foreign targets,
and, while it was opposed primarily by Republicans, it also received bipartisan
support.[129,130]

Our research implies that if what is past is prologue, congressional attention could once again temper excesses in the use of covert tools of statecraft.
Recent developments surrounding judicial rulings on presidential immunity,[131]
the expansive scope of executive authority, and the weakening of other institutional constraints on the presidency make the need for congressional vigilance
in overseeing intelligence and covert activities perhaps greater than ever. As
we show, formal oversight efforts can be complicated by high levels of partisan polarization and opposition politics but also – and more importantly –
by the ideological dispositions of the different parties, with one party being
especially likely to favor presidential discretion in such matters, regardless of
who sits in the Oval Office. While these dynamics make the bipartisan cooperation necessary for effective oversight more difficult, they do not completely
preclude it. Our research also indicates that Congress can constrain the president's use of these instruments even in the absence of appropriate oversight
instruments. To do so, legislators must be attentive, proactive, and willing to
flex their muscles and make use of the various tools at their disposal, as the
Executive often has the incentives, means, and willingness to find ways to skirt
formal legal instruments by exploiting loopholes and going as far as breaking
the law.

See also documents in Jeffrey T. Richelson, ed., "The Snowden Affair: Web Resource Documents the Latest Firestorm over the National Security Agency," National Security Archive
Electronic Briefing Book No. 436, posted September 4, 2013.

[129] The 2013 Amash-Conyers Amendment to the 2014 Defense Budget, targeting NSA bulk collection of phone records, was narrowly defeated in the House of Representatives despite having
bipartisan support and bipartisan opposition. Despite fierce opposition from the White House
and Democrats in the Senate Intelligence Committee including Feinstein, nearly 60% of House
Democrats voted in favor of the Amendment, compared to only 40% of Republicans.

[130] "How the NSA Spying Programs Have Changed Since Snowden." Frontline, Feb 9, 2015; The
Reporters Committee for Freedom of the Press. "Seven Years on, Congressional Oversight of
NSA Policies Is Still a Slog," November 16, 2020.

[131] See Howe, Amy "Justices rule Trump has some immunity from prosecution." SCOTUSblog,
Jul 1, 2024; Binder et al. (2024).

Appendix A
Modeling Congressional Attention

Using speaker-related information from Gentzkow et al. (2019), we briefly explore the correlates of congressional attention to intelligence as a proportion of all speeches on the floor of Congress. This cursory analysis helps validate the measure and provides further evidence that partisanship and institutional reform do not meaningfully explain the variation in attention. Together, these findings also alleviate potential concerns with endogeneity, multicollinearity, or post-treatment bias in the statistical models presented in Section 3 of the main text and Appendix B.

Our first theoretical expectation is that levels of attention among members of Congress would have increased in the years *preceding* the observed decline in covert activities. Moreover, the relationship between time and attention should not be linear. Third, we expect that congressional attention to covert action reflects broader struggles between the Executive and Congress and abuses of presidential authority, rather than purely an exercise in partisanship. As discussed in the main text, the relationship between partisanship and attention is probably time-varying, and *somewhat* independent from the effect of ideology, as more liberal members in both parties have historically been more likely to call attention to abuses in intelligence and because the period studies here covers a substantial partisan sorting along ideological lines.

A.1 Description of variables

- *Republican*: Coded 1 if the speaker is a Republican and 0 if the speaker is a Democrat. For this analysis we dropped all third-party and independent members of Congress.
- *Year*: Because we expect the relationship to be nonlinear, we include multiple splines (10 knot-points, to be precise.)
- *Senate*: Coded 1 if the speech was made on the floor of the Senate and 0 if made in the House of Representatives.
- *Conservative*: This is the first-dimension (Liberal-Conservative) score from DW-NOMINATE, from Lewis et al. (2019). A continuous measure with higher scores interpreted as more conservative and lower scores interpreted as more liberal.
- *Divided Government*: Coded 1 if the president does not have a majority in either chamber of Congress.
- *Republican President*: Coded 1 if the president is a Republican and 0 if the president is a Democrat.

- *Covert FIRC Count (1-year lag)*: A count of the number of covert FIRC operations initiated the year before.
- *Election Year*: Coded 1 if a nationwide election was held that year.
- *First-quarter Approval*: President's approval in the first quarter of the year.

A.2 Results and Robustness Tests

Tables A.1 and A.2 report the full results of the models estimating the correlates of *congressional attention*, mentioned in the main text. Table A.1 reports the results underlying Figure 4, which allows for an interaction between time and partisanship. Table A.3 builds on these findings and further probes two potential sources of endogeneity, namely the possibility that congressional attention to covert action oversight is driven by opposition politics under divided government and that it is driven by recent uses of covert action. As we suggest in the main text, we find no evidence for either claim. To the extent that there exists a correlation between divided government and our measure of congressional attention, that correlation is only visible (Table A.3, Model 3) in the *post-1974* period, rather than before. This is directly at odds with the notion that divided government only has an effect before the oversight reforms of the 1970s, but consistent with the growing polarization and ideological realignment after Vietnam noted in the main text. Moreover, we find (Table A.3, Models 4 and 5) that while divided government is positively correlated with attention under Republican presidents, it is negatively correlated with attention when the president is a Democrat.[1]

In all models, *Republican* and *Conservative* have negative and significant coefficients, while *Senate* has a positive coefficient. Figure 4 plots the predicted probabilities of a speech on intelligence from a model that allows for an interaction between partisanship and time. The two main reasons one could expect temporal variation in the effect of partisanship are partisan sorting and realignment that take place during this period[2] and opposition politics, as Democrats might be more likely to call attention to intelligence operations under Republican presidents and vice versa. We do not find much support for the latter. As explained next, we find some evidence for the former and little evidence for the latter.

As mentioned earlier, in Table A.3 we allowed for interaction effects between divided government and formal congressional oversight changes (post-1974)

---

[1] The year splines likely "soak up" some of the variance, but we find that results are very similar when using splines with fewer knots (degrees of freedom).

[2] On different dimensions of partisan sorting and realignment since the 1940s, see references in the footnote on page 28.

Table A.1 Correlates of attention to intelligence, Model 1

	DV: Mention of intelligence?
Republican	−0.151***
	(0.050)
Year spline 1	3.193***
	(0.477)
Year spline 2	1.425***
	(0.315)
Year spline 3	2.082***
	(0.361)
Year spline 4	3.538***
	(0.317)
Year spline 5	1.679***
	(0.331)
Year spline 6	4.349***
	(0.318)
Year spline 7	2.958***
	(0.323)
Year spline 8	4.189***
	(0.324)
Year spline 9	4.023***
	(0.324)
Year spline 10	3.244***
	(0.321)
Senate	0.073***
	(0.025)
Conservative (Nominate, Dimension 1)	−0.142**
	(0.069)
Constant	−8.717***
	(0.314)
Observations	1,779,710
Log Likelihood	−43,354.690

Note: $^*p<0.1$; $^{**}p<0.05$; $^{***}p<0.01$

(Table A.3, Model 3), divided government and the party of the president (Table A.3, Model 4) and between the party of the legislator and the party of the president (Table A.3, Model 5). We again find little support for the hypothesis that opposition politics under divided government drives attention to covert action.

Table A.2 Correlates of attention to intelligence, Model 2

Republican	1.955**
	(0.812)
Senate	0.081***
	(0.025)
Conservative (Nominate, Dimension 1)	−0.142**
	(0.070)
Year spline 1	3.987***
	(0.964)
Year spline 2	3.277***
	(0.687)
Year spline 3	3.474***
	(0.767)
Year spline 4	5.022***
	(0.717)
Year spline 5	3.291***
	(0.734)
Year spline 6	5.997***
	(0.722)
Year spline 7	3.923***
	(0.728)
Year spline 8	6.336***
	(0.728)
Year spline 9	4.978***
	(0.729)
Year spline 10	4.704***
	(0.726)
Republican * Year spline 1	−0.915
	(1.137)
Republican * Year spline 2	−2.813***
	(0.794)
Republican * Year spline 3	−2.095**
	(0.902)
Republican * Year spline 4	−2.057**
	(0.817)
Republican * Year spline 5	−2.787***
	(0.848)

Table A.2 *(Continued)*

Republican * Year spline 6	−2.568***
	(0.819)
Republican * Year spline 7	−0.864
	(0.826)
Republican * Year spline 8	−3.804***
	(0.829)
Republican * Year spline 9	−0.871
	(0.828)
Republican * Year spline 10	−2.109**
	(0.824)
Observations	1,779,710
Log Likelihood	−43,258.380

Note: $^*p<0.1$; $^{**}p<0.05$; $^{***}p<0.01$

Table A.3 More robustness tests, checking potential endogeneity with alternative hypotheses

	Mention of intelligence?		
	(3)	(4)	(5)
Conservative	−0.137*	−0.139**	−0.131*
(Nominate, Dimension 1)	(0.070)	(0.070)	(0.070)
Republican	−0.166***	−0.161***	−0.040
(Congressperson)	(0.051)	(0.051)	(0.063)
Senate	0.082***	0.084***	0.086***
	(0.025)	(0.025)	(0.025)
Q1 Presidential	0.003**	−0.001	0.001
Approval	(0.002)	(0.002)	(0.002)
Election Year	−0.007	0.004	0.003
	(0.030)	(0.030)	(0.030)
Number of Covert FIRCs,	−0.013	−0.007	−0.022**
1-year lag	(0.011)	(0.012)	(0.011)
Republican President	−0.061	−0.052	0.389**
	(0.184)	(0.179)	(0.164)
Divided Government	0.112	−2.549***	0.212
	(0.166)	(0.568)	(0.166)

Table A.3 *(Continued)*

Post-1974	−0.245	0.429***	0.412***
	(0.176)	(0.090)	(0.090)
Divided Government	0.648***		
*Post-1974	(0.148)		
GOP President		3.100***	
*Divided Government		(0.604)	
GOP Congressperson			−0.183***
*GOP President			(0.056)
Constant	−11.087***	5.228	−13.207***
	(2.046)	(4.136)	(1.993)
Observations	1,657,582	1,657,582	1,657,582
Log Likelihood	−41,796.360	−41,792.540	−41,800.590

Note: $^*p<0.1$; $^{**}p<0.05$; $^{***}p<0.01$
Not reported: Year cubic splines (10 knots).

For example, *divided government* has a positive correlation with *congressional attention* only in the post-1974 period and not before.[3] Challenging the partisan opposition hypothesis, we find that Republican legislators are no more likely than Democrats to speak out about intelligence matters under Democratic presidents, even though they are less likely to do so under Republican presidents. Republican attention to intelligence seems to outstrip Democratic attention during the Truman and Carter administrations, and also perhaps under George H. W. Bush (our data only covers his first year in office) but, importantly, not under Kennedy and Johnson, against the expectations of the partisan opposition hypothesis.

Similarly, we find that *divided government* has a positive correlation with *congressional attention* under Republican presidents (i.e. more Democrats than Republicans in Congress) but is *negatively* correlated with attention under Democratic presidents (more Republicans than Democrats in Congress). This is probably largely a function of the fact that *liberal Democrats* are overall more likely to speak out on the issue regardless of their opposition status. Moreover, this squares with our qualitative understanding of important events

---

[3] Even allowing for the possibility that differences were harder to detect in the pre-Hughes-Ryan period, when much of the discourse on intelligence happened behind closed doors, the correlation found for the post-1974 period still contradicts theories regarding the effect of formal oversight on the role of partisanship while supporting our contention that partisanship becomes more, rather than less important in the 1970s as a result of partisan sorting and the higher salience of matters related to intelligence and covert operations.

in this period. For example, it was Senator Fulbright, the ranking Democrat in the Senate Foreign Relations Committee, who emerged as one of the sharpest critics of covert intervention in Cuba in 1961 and who led the charge in a fairly thorough congressional inquiry into the Bay of Pigs fiasco. Despite his generally interventionist disposition, Fulbright also eventually soured on the Vietnam War and the intervention in the Dominican Republic during the Johnson administration. After initially fending sharper criticism from some of his more liberal Democratic colleagues like Wayne Morse and Mike Mansfield, Fulbright ultimately joined them in publicly antagonizing Johnson and calling for more accountability (Felten, 1995). Fulbright's reversal "sent a chill through the White House" (Dallek, 1998, 288). As we point out in the main text, this kind of co-partisan criticism is not only common, especially among Democrats, but it is also more likely to have an effect on national security policies.

We also find no consistent correlation between attention and presidential approval.[4] Nor do we find that recent FIRCs drive attention. This is consistent with our argument that congressional attention to covert action is not driven by the *number* of recent operations – most of which are unbeknownst to members of Congress – or even by failures per se, but by broader Executive-Legislative tensions and perceived abuses of executive power, many of which only become known well after the fact and have little to do with FIRC operations.

---

[4] In fact, the occasional correlations we do find have the opposite sign than would have been expected.

Appendix B
Modeling Covert FIRCs

B.1 Description of variables

- **DV**: *Onset* is coded 1 if the U.S. initiates a covert FIRC operation against that country and 0 otherwise.[1]
- **IV**: *Congressional Attention*. We used the estimates from the ten-topic model of intelligence speeches (see Section 3) to produce an indicator of congressional attention to intelligence oversight in a year by calculating the percentage of intelligence-related speeches relating to oversight. Congressional attention is, then, the *estimated percentage of speeches related to intelligence oversight* as a share of *all* congressional floor speeches in a given year. This produces a number that is bound between 0 and 1.
- **Domestic controls**: These are the domestic-level variables from Smith (2019). *Divided Government* is coded as 1 if the congressional majority is from a different party than the president's and 0 otherwise. *Election Year* is coded as 1 if it's a presidential election year. *Q1 Approval* is the President's mean approval for the first quarter of a given year, taken from Gallup polls (Smith, 2019, 698). We include president-fixed effects in the form of an indicator for each president from Truman to Carter, with Reagan-Bush being the excluded category. In other models, we dropped presidential dummies.
- **Dyadic and Target Controls**: *Relative capabilities* the target's capabilities (measured by the Correlates of War Composite Index of National Capabilities) as a share of US capabilities. *Democracy* is coded as 1 if the country is a democracy and 0 otherwise.[2] *Active Soviet Operation* is coded as 1 if the country is the target of an ongoing Soviet covert operation according to Berger et al. (2013).
- **Time controls**: *Peace years*, or the number of years since the last onset of a covert FIRC operation, and its squared and cubic terms (Carter and Signorino, 2010).

B.2 Results and Robustness Tests

Table B.1 reports the full results described and graphically displayed in the main text (Figure 7). Table B.2 reports the results of a series of robustness tests mentioned in Section 3. Some of the main findings are:

---

[1] The O'Rourke & Downes dataset includes both overt and covert FIRC operations, but as our theory deals with covert action, we only include the latter in our models.

[2] Regime type data is from Geddes et al. (2014).

Table B.1 Main models of covert foreign imposed regime change initiation

	(1) Base model	(2) Dom. controls	(3) Int. controls	(4) GLM time-series
Congr. Attention	−0.754**	−0.731*	−0.595†	−0.717*
	(−2.69)	(−2.29)	(−1.91)	(−2.13)
Divided Gov.		−0.448	−0.458	−0.292
		(−0.96)	(−0.90)	(−0.53)
Election Year		−0.0957	−0.270	−0.104
		(−0.24)	(−0.65)	(−0.23)
Pres. Approval		0.0355*	0.0261†	0.0445*
		(2.30)	(1.67)	(2.30)
USSR			1.512***	
Intervention			(4.40)	
Relative			−0.143	
Capabilities			(−1.45)	
Democratic			−0.473	
Target			(−1.23)	
Truman		−0.311	0.389	0.377
		(−0.41)	(0.49)	(0.62)
Eisenhower	−0.548	−1.490†	−0.900	−1.409*
	(−1.24)	(−1.91)	(−1.16)	(−1.99)
Kennedy	0.322	−1.212	−0.877	−1.088
	(0.68)	(−1.39)	(−0.95)	(−1.45)
Johnson	0.00245	−1.122	−0.876	−0.973
	(0.01)	(−1.35)	(−1.04)	(−1.39)
Nixon	−1.626*	−2.088*	−1.773*	−2.065*
	(−2.06)	(−2.34)	(−2.00)	(−2.52)
Ford	−0.156	0.299	0.0338	0.521
	(−0.17)	(0.29)	(0.03)	(0.45)
Carter	−0.0270	−1.020	−0.935	−0.883
	(−0.04)	(−1.33)	(−1.19)	(−0.87)
Reagan	0.542			
	(1.06)			
Constant	−3.827***	−5.030***	−5.332***	−6.500***
	(−9.19)	(−4.25)	(−4.02)	(−4.87)
Observations	5050	5050	5032	43

t statistics in parentheses.

Not reported: Peace-years cubic polynomials

†$p < 0.1$; *$p < 0.05$; **$p < 0.01$; ***$p < 0.001$.

Table B.2 Additional robustness tests

	B1	B2	B3	B4	B5	B6	B7	B8
Congr. Att. 20	−1.164†	−1.226*						
	(−1.87)	(−1.99)						
Congr. Att., 2y avg.			−0.560	−0.664†				
			(−1.51)	(−1.74)				
Congr. Att.					−0.481*	−0.578*	−0.605†	−0.676†
					(−2.15)	(−2.32)	(−1.84)	(−1.92)
Divided Gov.	−0.527	−0.386	−0.414	−0.270	−0.568†	−0.598	−0.464	−0.299
	(−1.01)	(−0.71)	(−0.80)	(−0.51)	(−1.87)	(−1.53)	(−0.91)	(−0.55)
Oversight Reforms							0.903	1.162
							(0.82)	(0.86)
Divided Gov. * Oversight Reforms							0.999	0.932
							(1.30)	(0.92)
USSR Intervention	1.515***		1.518***		1.525***		1.518***	
	(4.42)		(4.43)		(4.40)		(4.37)	
Rel. Capabilities	−0.144		−0.142		−0.150		−0.145	
	(−1.44)		(−1.44)		(−1.42)		(−1.46)	
Democratic Target	−0.484		−0.474		−0.343		−0.464	
	(−1.25)		(−1.23)		(−0.90)		(−1.20)	

	(1)	(2)	(3)	(4)	(5)	(6)	(7)	(8)
Election Year	−0.166	−0.0430	−0.313	−0.103	−0.320	−0.160	−0.291	−0.121
	(−0.38)	(−0.09)	(−0.79)	(−0.23)	(−0.91)	(−0.40)	(−0.70)	(−0.27)
Pres. Approval	0.0265†	0.0435*	0.0256	0.0437*	0.00615	0.0129	0.0232	0.0421*
	(1.73)	(2.24)	(1.54)	(2.20)	(0.50)	(0.90)	(1.48)	(2.19)
President Dummies	Yes	Yes	Yes	Yes	No	No	Constrained	Constrained
Constant	−4.315**	−5.289***	−5.310***	−6.427***	−4.159***	−5.032***	−6.967***	−8.410***
	(−3.05)	(−3.66)	(−3.83)	(−4.73)	(−4.68)	(−5.99)	(−4.40)	(−5.72)
Peace Years Polynomials	Yes	Yes	Yes	Yes	Yes	Yes	Yes	Yes
Constant	−4.315**	−5.289***	−5.310***	−6.427***	−5.310***	−6.427***	−6.967***	−8.410***
	(−3.05)	(−3.66)	(−3.83)	(−4.73)	(−3.83)	(−4.73)	(−4.40)	(−5.72)
N	5032	43	5032	43	5032	43	5032	43

t statistics in parentheses.

† $p < 0.1$; * $p < 0.05$; ** $p < 0.01$; *** $p < 0.001$.

- Models B1 and B2 repeat the analysis in Models 3 and 4, respectively, but use a measure of Congressional Attention resulting from a different topic model that breaks down intelligence-related speeches into twenty topics. The results are comparable and perhaps even stronger than the ones reported in the main model.
- Models B3 and B4 repeat the same analysis but take a two-year simple average of Congressional Attention. We expect the Executive can take some time to adjust to the constraints imposed by legislative attention and show qualitative evidence for this tendency in the manuscript. This might also ward off concerns regarding endogeneity, as heightened congressional attention could in part be a response to ongoing or past instances of covert action, though we find little evidence of this in Appendix A. We should note, however, that this kind of endogeneity would drastically attenuate our findings as that correlation between covert action and attention would be positive. The results lose some significance in some of the models, as can be expected by including such a wide window.
- Models B5 and B6 repeat models 3 and 4 in Table B.1, respectively, excluding presidential dummies.
- Models B7 and B8 test Smith's (2019) hypothesis regarding the effect of divided government conditional on oversight reform in both the panel and time-series form. The coefficient for divided government in these models should be interpreted as the coefficient for the years before 1975, the "year of intelligence." They are not statistically significant in either model. The coefficient on the interaction term is not statistically significant in these models (though we did find borderline significant results in a limited number of models), suggesting that the effect is at best only weakly conditional or that the conditional relationship found in the original study is spurious. The evidence accumulated in this paper favors the latter conclusion.
- Note on discrepancies between our findings and Smith (2019): The results we present in the main text cannot be considered direct replications, as we found a few errors including duplicates for observations and, consequently, incorrectly calculated peace-years. After correcting these errors, using Smith's full data and replication code, several results failed to replicate, with *divided government* losing statistical significance in the main models.

References

Abadie, Alberto, Susan Athey, Guido W Imbens, and Jeffrey Wooldridge (2017). When should you adjust standard errors for clustering? Technical report, National Bureau of Economic Research.

Almond, Gabriel A (1956). Public opinion and national security policy. *Public Opinion Quarterly 20*(2), 371–378.

Aronsson-Storrier, Marie (2020). *Publicity in international lawmaking: Covert operations and the use of force.* Cambridge University Press.

Balakrishnan, Nandita N (2020). *Where Have All the Coups Gone?* Ph.D. thesis, Stanford University.

Barkawi, Tarak (2015). Scientific decay. *International Studies Quarterly 59*(4), 827–829.

Barrett, David (2005). *The CIA and Congress: The untold story from Truman to Kennedy.* University Press of Kansas.

Baum, Matthew A and Tim Groeling (2009). Shot by the messenger: Partisan cues and public opinion regarding national security and war. *Political Behavior 31*(2), 157–186.

Berger, Daniel, William Easterly, Nathan Nunn, and Shanker Satyanath (2013). Commercial imperialism? Political influence and trade during the Cold War. *American Economic Review 103*(2), 863–896.

Biddle, Stephen, Jeffrey A Friedman, and Stephen Long (2012). Civil war intervention and the problem of Iraq. *International Studies Quarterly 56*(1), 85–98.

Binder, Sarah, James Goldgeier, and Elizabeth N Saunders (2024, July). The Imperial Presidency Unleashed. *Foreign Affairs.*

Boucher, Vincent and Frédérick Gagnon (2024). Partisanship and congressional intelligence oversight: The case of the Russia inquiries, 2017–2020. *Intelligence and National Security 39*(1), 19–39.

Brands, William J (1969). Intelligence and foreign policy: Dilemmas of a democracy. *Foreign Affairs 47*(2), 281–295.

Bueno De Mesquita, Bruce and George W Downs (2006). Intervention and democracy. *International Organization 60*(3), 627–649.

Carnegie, Allison and Austin Carson (2020). *Secrets in global governance: Disclosure dilemmas and the challenge of international cooperation,* Volume 154. Cambridge University Press.

Carson, Austin (2018). *Secret wars.* Princeton University Press.

Carter, David B and Curtis S Signorino (2010). Back to the future: Modeling time dependence in binary data. *Political Analysis 18*(3), 271–292.

Chafetz, Josh (2017). *Congress's constitution: Legislative authority and the separation of powers*. Yale University Press.

Charlton, Linda (1975, June). Nedzi's Critic to Head C.I.A. Inquiry. *The New York Times*.

Clark, Tom S (2009). Measuring ideological polarization on the United States supreme court. *Political Research Quarterly 62*(1), 146–157.

Colaresi, Michael P (2014). *Democracy declassified: The secrecy dilemma in national security*. Oxford University Press.

Committee on Foreign Affairs House of Representatives (1987). Possible violation or circumvention of the Clark Amendment. Hearing before the Subcommittee on Africa, One Hundredth Congress, first session, Wednesday, July 1.

Cormac, Rory and Richard J Aldrich (2018). Grey is the new black: Covert action and implausible deniability. *International Affairs 94*(3), 477–494.

Cormac, Rory, Calder Walton, and Damien Van Puyvelde (2022). What constitutes successful covert action? Evaluating unacknowledged interventionism in foreign affairs. *Review of International Studies 48*(1), 111–128.

Cramer, Jane Kellett (2006, January). "Just cause" or just politics?: U.S. Panama invasion and standardizing qualitative tests for diversionary war. *Armed Forces & Society 32*(2), 178–201.

Crawford, Mark (1987). Glenn asks Reagan to halt Pakistan aid pending review of nuclear programs. *Science 235*(4794), 1321–1321.

Crile, George (2003). *Charlie Wilson's war*. Grove Press.

Cumming, Alfred (2011, April). Sensitive Covert Action Notifications: Oversight Options for Congress. Archive Location: United States Publisher: Library of Congress. Congressional Research Service.

Dallek, Robert (1998). *Flawed giant: Lyndon Johnson and his times, 1961–1973*. Oxford University Press.

Davies, Graeme AM and Robert Johns (2013). Audience costs among the British public: The impact of escalation, crisis type, and prime ministerial rhetoric. *International Studies Quarterly 57*(4), 725–737.

DeLaet, C James and James M Scott (2006). Treaty-making and partisan politics: Arms control and the US senate, 1960–2001. *Foreign Policy Analysis 2*(2), 177–200.

Dinges, John (1990). *Our man in Panama: How General Noriega Used the United States and made millions in drugs and arms*. Random House Incorporated.

Downes, Alexander B (2021). *Catastrophic success*. Cornell University Press.

Downes, Alexander B and Lindsey A O'Rourke (2016). You can't always get what you want: Why foreign-imposed regime change seldom improves interstate relations. *International Security 41*(2), 43–89.

Druckman, James N, Erik Peterson, and Rune Slothuus (2013). How elite partisan polarization affects public opinion formation. *American Political Science Review 107*(1), 57–79.

Durbin, Brent (2017). *The CIA and the politics of US intelligence reform.* Cambridge University Press.

Eason, Thomas, Oliver Daddow, and Rory Cormac (2020). From secrecy to accountability: The politics of exposure in the Belgrano affair. *The British Journal of Politics and International Relations 22*(3), 542–560.

Edwards, George C (2006). *On deaf ears: The limits of the bully pulpit.* Yale University Press.

Engelberg, Stephen (1989, October). Reagan Agreed to Prevent Noriega Death. *The New York Times.*

Fearon, James D (1994). Domestic political audiences and the escalation of international disputes. *American Political Science Review 88*(3), 577–592.

Felten, Peter Gerhard (1995). *The 1965–1966 United States Intervention in the Dominican Republic.* Ph. D. thesis, The University of Texas at Austin.

Fordham, Benjamin O (2002). Another look at "parties, voters, and the use of force abroad." *Journal of Conflict Resolution 46*(4), 572–596.

Fowler, Linda L (2015). *Watchdogs on the hill: The decline of congressional oversight of US foreign relations.* Princeton University Press.

Foyle, Douglas C (1997). Public opinion and foreign policy: Elite beliefs as a mediating variable. *International Studies Quarterly 41*(1), 141–169.

Franck, Edward and Thomas M. & Weisband (1979). *Foreign Policy by Congress.* New York: Oxford University Press.

Friedberg, Aaron L (2000). *In the shadow of the garrison state: America's anti-statism and its Cold War grand strategy.* Princeton University Press.

Friedrichs, Gordon M and Jordan Tama (2022). Polarization and US foreign policy: Key debates and new findings. *International Politics 59*(5), 767–785.

Froio, Caterina, Shaun Bevan, and Will Jennings (2017). Party mandates and the politics of attention: Party platforms, public priorities and the policy agenda in Britain. *Party Politics 23*(6), 692–703.

Geddes, Barbara, Joseph Wright, and Erica Frantz (2014). Autocratic breakdown and regime transitions: A new data set. *Perspectives on Politics 12*(2), 313–331.

Gentzkow, Matthew, Bryan Kelly, and Matt Taddy (2019). Text as data. *Journal of Economic Literature 57*(3), 535–574.

Gerring, John (2006). *Case study research: Principles and practices*. Cambridge University Press.

Gleijeses, Piero (2013). *Visions of freedom: Havana, Washington, Pretoria, and the struggle for Southern Africa, 1976–1991*. UNC Press Books.

Goldman, Minton F (1992). President Bush and Afghanistan: A turning point in American policy. *Comparative Strategy 11*(2), 177–193.

Gowa, Joanne (1998). Politics at the water's edge: Parties, voters, and the use of force abroad. *International Organization 52*(2), 307–324.

Gries, Peter (2020). *The politics of American foreign policy: How ideology divides liberals and conservatives over foreign affairs*. Stanford University Press.

Guisinger, Alexandra and Elizabeth N Saunders (2017). Mapping the boundaries of elite cues: How elites shape mass opinion across international issues. *International Studies Quarterly 61*(2), 425–441.

Haas, Melinda (2023). Origins of oversight: Covert action amendments to the national security act of 1947. *International Journal of Intelligence and CounterIntelligence 36*(4), 1297–1318.

Haines, Gerald K (2004). Looking for a rogue elephant: The Pike Committee investigations and the CIA. In S. Chauhan (Ed.), *Inside CIA: Lessons in Intelligence*, pp. 272–283. APH Publishing.

Halliday, Fred (1983). *The making of the Second Cold War*. Verso.

Hampson, Fen Osler (1984). The divided decision-maker: American domestic politics and the Cuban crises. *International Security 9*(3), 130–165.

Hathaway, Robert M and Russell Jack Smith (1993). *Richard Helms as Director of Central Intelligence 1966–1973*. History Staff, Center for the Study of Intelligence, Central Intelligence Agency.

Hayes, Jarrod (2012). Securitization, social identity, and democratic security: Nixon, India, and the ties that bind. *International Organization 66*(1), 63–93.

Heymann, Philip B (2008). *Living the policy process*. Oxford University Press.

Hoffman, David and John M. Goshko (1989, October). Administration Sought Funds Last Spring for Covert Action. *Washington Post*.

Holsti, Ole R (1992). Public opinion and foreign policy: Challenges to the Almond-Lippmann consensus. *International studies quarterly 36*(4), 439–466.

Holsti, Ole R (2004). *Public opinion and American foreign policy*. University of Michigan Press.

Hosmer, Stephen T (2001). *Operations against enemy leaders*. Rand Corporation.

Howard, Lise Morjé and Alexandra Stark (2018). How civil wars end: The international system, norms, and the role of external actors. *International Security 42*(3), 127–171.

Howell, William G and Jon C Pevehouse (2007). *While dangers gather: Congressional checks on presidential war powers*. Princeton University Press.

Hughes, Tyler (2018). Assessing minority party influence on partisan issue attention in the US house of representatives, 1989–2012. *Party Politics 24*(2), 197–208.

Jeffreys-Jones, Rhodri (2003). *The CIA & American democracy*. Yale University Press.

Jeong, Gyung-Ho and Paul J Quirk (2019). Division at the water's edge: The polarization of foreign policy. *American Politics Research 47*(1), 58–87.

Johnson, Loch K (1989). Covert action and accountability: Decision-making for America's secret foreign policy. *International Studies Quarterly 33*(1), 81–109.

Johnson, Loch K (2005). Accountability and America's secret foreign policy: Keeping a legislative eye on the Central Intelligence Agency. *Foreign Policy Analysis 1*(1), 99–120.

Johnson, Loch K (2017). *Spy watching: Intelligence accountability in the United States*. Oxford University Press.

Jones, Bryan D and Frank R Baumgartner (2004). Representation and agenda setting. *Policy Studies Journal 32*(1), 1–24.

Joseph, Michael F and Michael Poznansky (2018). Media technology, covert action, and the politics of exposure. *Journal of Peace Research 55*(3), 320–335.

Krasner, Stephen D (2009). *Power, the state, and sovereignty: Essays on international relations*. Routledge.

Kreps, Sarah (2010). Elite consensus as a determinant of alliance cohesion: Why public opinion hardly matters for NATO-led operations in Afghanistan. *Foreign Policy Analysis 6*(3), 191–215.

Kreps, Sarah and Debak Das (2017). Warring from the virtual to the real: Assessing the public's threshold for war over cyber security. *Research & Politics 4*(2), 2053168017715930.

Kriner, Douglas and Eric Schickler (2018). The resilience of separation of powers? Congress and the Russia investigation. *Presidential Studies Quarterly 48*(3), 436–455.

Kriner, Douglas L (2010). *After the Rubicon: Congress, presidents, and the politics of waging war*. University of Chicago Press.

Kriner, Douglas L (2018). Congress, public opinion, and an informal constraint on the commander-in-chief. *The British Journal of Politics and International Relations 20*(1), 52–68.

Kupchan, Charles A and Peter L Trubowitz (2007). Dead center: The demise of liberal internationalism in the United States. *International Security 32*(2), 7–44.

Kuperman, Alan J (1999). The stinger missile and US intervention in Afghanistan. *Political Science Quarterly 114*(2), 219–263.

Kuperman, Alan J (2008). The moral hazard of humanitarian intervention: Lessons from the Balkans. *International Studies Quarterly 52*(1), 49–80.

Lang, Corey and Shanna Pearson-Merkowitz (2015). Partisan sorting in the United States, 1972–2012: New evidence from a dynamic analysis. *Political Geography 48*, 119–129.

Leary, William M (1984). *The Central Intelligence Agency: History and documents*. University of Alabama Press.

Lee, Frances E (2009). *Beyond ideology: Politics, principles, and partisanship in the US Senate*. University of Chicago Press.

Lee, Frances E (2016). *Insecure majorities: Congress and the perpetual campaign*. University of Chicago Press.

Lester, Genevieve (2015). *When should state secrets stay secret?: Accountability, democratic governance, and intelligence*. Cambridge University Press.

Lester, Genevieve and Frank Leith Jones (2021). Reaching the inflection point: The Hughes-Ryan Amendment and intelligence oversight. In *National security intelligence and ethics*, pp. 201–215. Routledge.

Levin, Dov H (2016). When the great power gets a vote: The effects of great power electoral interventions on election results. *International Studies Quarterly 60*(2), 189–202.

Lewis, Jeffrey B, Keith Poole, Howard Rosenthal, et al. (2019). Voteview: Congressional Roll-Call Votes Database. *See https://voteview. com/*.

Lindsay, James M (1994). *Congress and the politics of US foreign policy*. JHU Press.

Lippmann, Walter (1946). *Public opinion*, Volume 1. New York: Start.

Mason, Lilliana (2015). "I disrespectfully agree": The differential effects of partisan sorting on social and issue polarization. *American Journal of Political Science 59*(1), 128–145.

Mayhew, David R (2000). Electoral realignments. *Annual Review of Political Science 3*(1), 449–474.

McCubbins, Mathew D and Thomas Schwartz (1984). Congressional oversight overlooked: Police patrols versus fire alarms. *American Journal of Political Science 28*(1), 165–179.

McFaul, Michael (1989). Rethinking the "Reagan doctrine" in Angola. *International Security 14*(3), 99–135.

Milner, Helen V and Dustin Tingley (2015). *Sailing the water's edge: The domestic politics of American foreign policy.* Princeton University Press.

Moran, Christopher (2015). Turning against the CIA: Whistleblowers during the "time of troubles." *History 100*(340), 251–274.

Moynihan, Daniel Patrick (1998). *Secrecy: The American experience.* Yale University Press.

Murdie, Amanda and Dursun Peksen (2014). The impact of human rights INGO shaming on humanitarian interventions. *The Journal of Politics 76*(1), 215–228.

Noel, Hans (2012). The coalition merchants: The ideological roots of the civil rights realignment. *The Journal of Politics 74*(1), 156–173.

O'Rourke, Lindsey A (2018). *Covert regime change: America's secret Cold War.* Cornell University Press.

Page, Benjamin I and Robert Y Shapiro (2010). *The rational public: Fifty years of trends in Americans' policy preferences.* University of Chicago Press.

Painter, David (2002). *The Cold War: An international history.* Routledge.

Peck, Justin C and Jeffery A Jenkins (2020). The "flip-side" of delegation: Examining congressional reassertion efforts. In J. L. Carson and M. S. Lynch (Eds.), *New directions in Congressional politics*, pp. 251–273. Routledge.

Peksen, Dursun (2011). Foreign military intervention and women's rights. *Journal of Peace Research 48*(4), 455–468.

Petersen, Roger D (2011). *Western intervention in the Balkans: The strategic use of emotion in conflict.* Cambridge University Press.

Pickering, Jeffrey and Emizet F Kisangani (2009). The international military intervention dataset: An updated resource for conflict scholars. *Journal of Peace Research 46*(4), 589–599.

Poznansky, Michael (2015). Stasis or decay? Reconciling covert war and the democratic peace. *International Studies Quarterly 59*(4), 815–826.

Poznansky, Michael (2020). *In the shadow of international law: Secrecy and regime change in the postwar world.* Oxford University Press.

Poznansky, Michael, Alexander B Downes, and Lindsey A O'Rourke (2017). Friends, foes, and foreign-imposed regime change. *International Security 42*(2), 191–195.

Prados, John (2003). *Lost crusader: The secret wars of CIA Director William Colby.* Oxford University Press.

Prados, John (2006). *Safe for democracy: The secret wars of the CIA.* Ivan R. Dee.

Quinn, Kevin M, Burt L Monroe, Michael Colaresi, Michael H Crespin, and Dragomir R Radev (2010). How to analyze political attention with minimal assumptions and costs. *American Journal of Political Science 54*(1), 209–228.

Rielly, John E. (1975). *American Public Opinion and U.S. foreign policy*, 1975. Chicago Council on Foreign Relations.

Rio Tinto, Daniel (2017). *Tracing the security dilemma in civil wars: How fear and insecurity can lead to intra-state violence*. Ph. D. thesis, University of Birmingham.

Risse-Kappen, Thomas (1991). Public opinion, domestic structure, and foreign policy in liberal democracies. *World politics 43*(4), 479–512.

Roberts, Margaret E, Brandon M Stewart, and Dustin Tingley (2019). Stm: An R package for structural topic models. *Journal of Statistical Software 91*(1), 1–40.

Robinson, Linda (1988). Dwindling options in panama. *Foreign Affairs 68*, 187.

Rohde, David W (1991). *Parties and leaders in the postreform House*. University of Chicago Press.

Ross-Nazzal, Jennifer (2010). Détente on Earth and in space: The Apollo-Soyuz test project. *Organization of American Historians Magazine of History 24*(3), 29–34.

Saunders, Elizabeth N (2009). Transformative choices: Leaders and the origins of intervention strategy. *International Security 34*(2), 119–161.

Saunders, Elizabeth N (2012). The electoral disconnection in US foreign policy. In *APSA 2012 Annual Meeting Paper*.

Saunders, Elizabeth N (2015). War and the inner circle: Democratic elites and the politics of using force. *Security Studies 24*(3), 466–501.

Saunders, Elizabeth N (2024). *The insiders' game: How elites make war and peace*, Volume 207. Princeton University Press.

Schickler, Eric (2016). *Racial realignment: The transformation of American liberalism, 1932–1965*. Princeton University Press.

Schlesinger, Arthur M (2004). *The imperial presidency*. HMH.

Schultz, Kenneth A (2001). *Democracy and coercive diplomacy*, Volume 76. Cambridge University Press.

Seawright, Jason (2016). *Multi-method social science: Combining qualitative and quantitative tools*. Cambridge University Press.

Sinclair, Barbara (2014, December). *Congressional realignment, 1925–1978*. University of Texas Press.

Smith, Gregory L (2019). Secret but constrained: The impact of elite opposition on covert operations. *International Organization 73*(3), 685–707.

Snider, L Britt (2015). *The agency and the hill.* Government Printing Office.

Snyder, Jack, Robert Y Shapiro, and Yaeli Bloch-Elkon (2009). Free hand abroad, divide and rule at home. *World Politics 61*(1), 155–187.

Tama, Jordan (2020). Forcing the president's hand: How the US congress shapes foreign policy through sanctions legislation. *Foreign Policy Analysis 16*(3), 397–416.

Tama, Jordan (2024). *Bipartisanship and US foreign policy: Cooperation in a polarized age.* Oxford University Press.

Theoharis, Athan G, Richard H Immerman, Kathryn Olmsted, and John Prados (2005). *The Central Intelligence Agency: Security under scrutiny.* Bloomsbury Publishing.

Touchton, Michael R, Casey A Klofstad, Jonathan P West, and Joseph E Uscinski (2020, January). Whistleblowing or leaking? Public opinion toward Assange, Manning, and Snowden. *Research & Politics 7*(1), 1–9.

United States Congress Senate Committee on Foreign Relations (1960, May 27). *Events Incident to the Summit Conference: Hearings before the Committee on Foreign Relations, United States Senate, Eighty-Sixth Congress, Second Session.* U.S. Government Printing Office.

Weeks, Jessica L (2008). Autocratic audience costs: Regime type and signaling resolve. *International Organization 62*(1), 35–64.

Weisberg, Herbert F (2002). The party in the electorate as a basis for more responsible parties. *Responsible Partisanship,* 161–179.

Wells, Matthew S and Timothy J Ryan (2018). Following the party in time of war? The implications of elite consensus. *International Interactions 44*(5), 919–935.

Westad, Odd Arne (2005). *The global Cold War: Third World interventions and the making of our times.* Cambridge University Press.

Wheeler, Nicholas J (2000). *Saving strangers: Humanitarian intervention in international society.* OUP Oxford.

Wittkopf, Eugene R (1990). *Faces of internationalism: Public opinion and American foreign policy.* Duke University Press.

Wohlforth, William C (2020). Realism and great power subversion. *International Relations 34*(4), 459–481.

Zegart, Amy and Julie Quinn (2010). Congressional intelligence oversight: The electoral disconnection. *Intelligence and National Security 25*(6), 744–766.

Zegart, Amy B (2000). *Flawed by design: The evolution of the CIA, JCS, and NSC.* Stanford University Press.

Zegart, Amy B (2011). The domestic politics of irrational intelligence oversight. *Political Science Quarterly 126*(1), 1–25.

Zegart, Amy B (2013). *Eyes on spies: Congress and the United States intelligence community.* Hoover Press.

Acknowledgments

This manuscript had a long gestation period. It was originally conceived in 2013, and the research was conducted while the authors were housed at various institutions, including Georgetown, Yale, MIT, Boston College, Notre Dame, Carnegie Mellon, the US Army War College, and the University of Toronto. Early versions were presented at the International Studies Association Annual Conference, the American Political Science Association Annual Conference, the virtual conference on "International Relations and America's Rise: Institutions, Ideas, and Individuals" at the University of Chicago, as well as working paper seminars at several of our home institutions over the years. We want to thank especially: the Cambridge Elements lead editor, Jon Pevehouse, and the editorial team and anonymous reviewers; colleagues who read the manuscript particularly closely or more than once (John Chin, Dan Hansen, Dan Silverman, Marika Landau-Wells, Hope Dancy, Austin Carson, Andy Bennett, Robert Lieber, Nandita Balakrishnan, and Dov Levin) as well as student research assistants who helped with various important tasks over the years (Abigale Pfingsten, Arianna Garcia Guerrero, and Andey Ng).

Cambridge Elements ☰

International Relations

Series Editors

Jon C. W. Pevehouse
University of Wisconsin–Madison

Jon C. W. Pevehouse is the Mary Herman Rubinstein Professor of Political Science and Public Policy at the University of Wisconsin–Madison. He has published numerous books and articles in IR in the fields of international political economy, international organizations, foreign policy analysis, and political methodology. He is a former editor of the leading IR field journal, International Organization.

Tanja A. Börzel
Freie Universität Berlin

Tanja A. Börzel is the Professor of political science and holds the Chair for European Integration at the Otto-Suhr-Institute for Political Science, Freie Universität Berlin. She holds a PhD from the European University Institute, Florence, Italy. She is coordinator of the Research College "The Transformative Power of Europe," as well as the FP7-Collaborative Project "Maximizing the Enlargement Capacity of the European Union" and the H2020 Collaborative Project "The EU and Eastern Partnership Countries: An Inside-Out Analysis and Strategic Assessment." She directs the Jean Monnet Center of Excellence "Europe and its Citizens."

Edward D. Mansfield
University of Pennsylvania

Edward D. Mansfield is the Hum Rosen Professor of Political Science, University of Pennsylvania. He has published well over 100 books and articles in the area of international political economy, international security, and international organizations. He is Director of the Christopher H. Browne Center for International Politics at the University of Pennsylvania and former program co-chair of the American Political Science Association.

Editorial Team

International Relations Theory
Jeffrey T. Checkel, European University Institute, Florence

International Political Economy
Edward D. Mansfield, University of Pennsylvania
Stefanie Walter, University of Zurich

International Organisations
Tanja A. Börzel, Freie Universität Berlin
Jon C. W. Pevehouse, University of Wisconsin–Madison

About the Series

The Cambridge Elements Series in International Relations publishes original research on key topics in the field. The series includes manuscripts addressing international security, international political economy, international organizations, and international relations.

Cambridge Elements ⁼

International Relations

Elements in the Series

Printed in the United States
by Baker & Taylor Publisher Services